Reaching Out Through Christian Education

Steve Clapp and Jerry O. Cook

**ANDREW
CENTER
RESOURCES**

Reaching Out Through Christian Education

Steve Clapp and Jerry O. Cook

Biblical quotations, unless otherwise noted, are from the New Revised Standard Version of the Bible, copyrighted 1989 by the Division of Christian Education, National Council of Churches, and are used by permission.

ISBN 0-9637206-4-3

Manufactured in the United States of America

This book is dedicated to all the people who have invited us into their churches and participated in the surveys and interviews which have enabled us to better understand effective strategies for outreach. Our prayer is that the pages which follow will help many others in their efforts to reach out in the name of our Lord.

We express our special appreciation for the vital contributions made to this book by: Paul Mundey, Barb Faga, Karen Carlson, Carolyn Egolf, Holly Carcione, Jerry Peterson, and the staff of Evangel Press.

CONTENTS

INTRODUCTION.. 7

PART ONE:
REACHING OUT WITH INTENTIONALITY........................... 9

EVERYTHING TEACHES SOMETHING................................... 11

A FALSE TENSION: EVANGELISM VS. JUSTICE.................. 18

WHAT IS IT LIKE TO VISIT YOUR CHURCH?....................... 22

EVALUATING AND DREAMING.. 30

CURRICULUM IN A MEDIA DOMINATED AGE...................... 35

A RANGE OF METHODS... 41

PART TWO:
REACHING OUT THROUGH LEADERSHIP........................... 49

ADD LEADERS BEFORE ADDING STUDENTS....................... 51

RECRUITING TEACHERS AND GROUP LEADERS................. 55

TEACHER TRAINING, SUPPORT, AND REINFORCEMENT...... 62

JOB DESCRIPTIONS HELP EVERYONE WITH OUTREACH... 70

EMPLOYED STAFF AND CHRISTIAN EDUCATION................. 77

PART THREE:
REACHING OUT BY BUILDING ATTENDANCE..................... 81

MAINTAIN THOSE LISTS!... 83

KEEP THEM COMING... 84

GETTING THE WORD OUT.. 91

ATTENDANCE AND PARTICIPATION AWARDS........................ 98

VACATION BIBLE SCHOOL.. 103

TEACHING PEOPLE TO SHARE THEIR FAITH....................... 106

PART FOUR:
REACHING OUT TO PARTICULAR GROUPS..................... 113

THE LESSON OF THE SAMARITAN.................................. 115

YOUNG ADULTS AND THE PUSH FOR CHANGE................. 119

THE DIVORCED AND OTHERS NEEDING SUPPORT.......... 125

THOSE FACING DIFFICULT CHALLENGES........................ 131

REACHING TEENAGERS.. 137

RESOURCES.. 142

ABOUT THE AUTHORS... 144

In the presence of God and of Christ Jesus, who is to judge the living and the dead, and in view of his appearing and his kingdom, I solemnly urge you: proclaim the message; be persistent whether the time is favorable or unfavorable; convince, rebuke, and encourage, with the utmost patience in teaching.

2 Timothy 4:1-2

Introduction

The nurse who brought my breakfast also brought a warning: "I wouldn't be expecting company today. The highways are treacherous with ice, and another blizzard is on the way."

Great. Just great. I was ten years old and was spending the first part of Christmas vacation in the hospital. Doctors have a marvelous way of keeping most people from being hospitalized over the holidays, but they hadn't been successful in my case.

The pediatrics ward was a lonely place. I saw my parents each day, but I was feeling well enough that I wanted more company and more entertainment. My hometown was forty miles away, so the gloomy report of the nurse eliminated my hope that three friends were coming. Their parents would not bring them if the roads were hazardous. I didn't want them to take any chances, but I was lonely and felt sorry for myself.

But that day did bring a visitor in addition to my parents. My Sunday school teacher came to bring me a bag of candy and my Bible story paper for the week. Her husband had not wanted her to come, but she made the trip. She wanted me to know that she cared about me; that she was praying for me; and that I should be reading my Bible even if I couldn't come to class!

I ate the candy shortly after she left. In time, I threw away the Bible story paper. I never forgot the visit. The trip had been a hard one for her, and she stayed only a few minutes; but it was long enough for me to know that she cared. She cared about me, and she cared about the Bible and Christ. That day I started looking at the Bible with new respect, and I attended her Sunday school class with greater commitment.

She was one of many people who have nurtured me in the Christian faith. Her impact was especially important, because I remembered her concern and example long after I had forgotten much of the specific content from her class.

I have often used that story from my own life to open workshops on Christian education, and I always find that those who are in attendance have similar stories to share. The Christian education program of the local congregation has tremendous power to renew the church and to reach out to persons outside the church.

In this book, my good friend Jerry Cook and I share a range of effective strategies to help the local church:

- experience renewal through the Christian education program. Better procedures and improved leadership development are necessary if meaningful outreach is going to occur.

- utilize Christian education as a means to better motivate and equip the whole church for outreach.

- develop specific strategies which will reach out to persons who are inactive members and who are nonmembers.

- explore new ways of involving every age level in service to those in need.

Jerry and I have both spent years working in Christian education and youth ministry, and we've had the pleasure of observing the practices which have brought the best results in churches of many different denominations. Because each congregation and the community which it serves are unique, not every suggestion offered in the pages which follow will work in every setting; but you should find plenty of material which will be of use to you and which will stimulate your own thinking.

Steve Clapp

Part One:

Reaching Out
With Intentionality

Every aspect of the life of a Christian community educates (or miseducates) the faith of its members (and its "neighbors" as well!).

Thomas H. Groome
Boston College

Everything Teaches Something

> **Concept:** The greeters, the songs, the prayers, the sermon, the teachers, the classrooms, the hallways, the restrooms, the parking lot, and the newsletter are all part of the church's educational ministry. Every part of the life of the church teaches members and nonmembers something about the Christian faith, the church, and the church's concern for people.

Because I wanted to visit some friends I hadn't seen in years, I arrived in a large city the weekend before I was scheduled to do a consultation in a twelve hundred member church. To protect the guilty, I'll not mention the name of the city, the church, or the denomination.

On Saturday evening, I decided to abandon my friends long enough the next day to experience worship and Sunday school at the church I would be seeking to help later in the week. No one was expecting me until Monday evening; and I had not personally met the staff member who arranged the consultation, so I had the opportunity to truly view the church through the eyes of a visitor. I wasn't sure about the Sunday morning schedule and could not find it in the yellow pages, so I phoned one of the church's pastors around nine o'clock Saturday evening to ask for that information. I did not identify myself as the person who would be doing the consultation.

Few pastors like to have Saturday evening interrupted by the telephone, and this pastor was no exception. He didn't complain about my having called him at home, but he was abrupt and hung up the phone just as soon as he had shared worship and Sunday school times. If I'd wanted to ask for directions, I would have had to make another call.

The church was just off a major street, and some attractive signs in good repair guided me from that street to the building. The church parking lot was already full when I arrived, but I noticed a large, almost empty lot across the street. Unfortunately there was no sign that indicated it was available for church parking, but there was a huge sign which proclaimed:

> RESERVED PARKING
> 24 HOURS A DAY
> VIOLATORS WILL BE TOWED

That kind of sign reinforced the paranoia I've had since the winter day I parked in a music director's spot in a snow packed church lot that had nothing else available and returned from a visit with the senior pastor to discover that the church had towed my car away. (And, yes, I had told the church secretary that I was in someone else's spot; but she unfortunately did not communicate that to the overly efficient custodial staff of that congregation.)

I watched the almost empty lot for a few minutes and was relieved when three other drivers parked their cars there and then headed on foot for the church. I parked beside one of their cars.

I received a courteous, friendly greeting as I entered the church, and I was given good directions to a men's restroom located in the basement. When I walked into the restroom, I was a little disappointed to see some paint chipping on the outside wall and to detect an unpleasant odor from the two toilets. Perhaps that should have been a warning.

When I flushed the toilet, I almost went swimming. The water level rose so fast that the toilet overflowed before I could adjust the "float mechanism" (or whatever the correct name is for the device that has to be pulled up to stop the flow of water). Water got on the floor and on my shoes.

I went back to the friendly greeter to report that there was a problem with one of the toilets. He apologized and asked me if I would go to the church office and tell someone on the staff.

That gave me the opportunity to meet a pastor I had not phoned the night before. He was in a hurry and apparently assumed that I was a member of the congregation. Rather than reassuring me that something would be done about it and thanking me for reporting it, he gave me directions to the supply closet and suggested that I mop up the water.

I have mopped up water in churches on other occasions, and I'm sure that I will in the future. It's an odd experience as a visitor, however, to be told to clean up a restroom. I was obedient. I did it.

That made me arrive a few minutes late for an adult Sunday school class which the greeter had suggested to me. There were around twenty-five people in the group - primarily, but not exclusively, couples. They were sharing coffee as I entered, and the class president poured a cup for me and introduced me to others. I used only my first name to preserve my role as visitor.

When the lecture and discussion portion of the class began, I was struck by the reality that only three people often had anything to say, and they were always in agreement with the teacher, despite the fact that the topic under discussion, abortion, is one which usually generates a range of opinions. I decided to play devil's advocate by taking the opposite position in order to see what the response would be. After I expressed my opinion, the teacher spoke to me in a condescending tone: "Well, son, the view you're expressing is an immature one. When you've been around as long as some of us have, then you'll understand why you're wrong." That's the kind of response that makes a visitor want to bolt out of the classroom and never return.

The worship service which I attended following the Sunday school class was, on the whole, well conducted. The sermon was a well-crafted explanation and application of 1 Corinthians 13. Participation for a visitor would have been a little easier if the bulletin had indicated whether members of that congregation were debtors, sinners, or trespassers as far as the Lord's Prayer is concerned.

Steve Clapp is the coauthor whose church visit has just been described. He learned a great many things from preparation for the Sunday morning visit and from the visit itself:

- That at least one of the pastors didn't hesitate to give a cold response to a Saturday night phone call seeking church information. The church could have made that information available through the yellow pages advertisement or through a recorded message on the church's phone line so that staff would not have to be called. If called, however, staff should not give a cold response to a visitor and perhaps even potential member.

• That the church has taken care to have signs which give good directions to the building only to fail to have any sign indicating that Sunday morning parking was permitted in the lot across the street. [Steve's car did not get towed.]

• That the greeter, at the entrance used, had probably received some training in how to direct people to classes as well as to restrooms, and that the greeter had a warm personality.

• That pride in the church apparently did not extend to the condition of the basement men's restroom. (It also turned out that the nursery restrooms also had some peeling paint, which would be a major concern for any parent who noticed.)

• That the pastor in the office apparently did not know the membership of the church well enough to distinguish between a member and a visitor (though that is a difficult task in such a large congregation), and that he felt no reluctance to ask a person he did not know to mop the restroom floor.

• That the class which was visited was glad enough to have a visitor as long as it appeared that the visitor was in agreement with the opinions of the teacher and the dominant class members.

Thomas Groome, author of *Christian Religious Education* and of *Sharing Faith*, writes that: "Every aspect of the life of a Christian community educates (or miseducates) the faith of its members (and its 'neighbors' as well!)." How true those words are! A comprehensive definition of Christian education can in fact end up including everything which happens in the life of the church. Sunday school, parochial school, CCD classes, confirmation classes, small groups, and youth groups have traditionally been viewed as Christian education. It's also true, however, that the sermon, the hymns, the prayers, and every other aspect of services of worship have strong Christian

14

education functions. The way the physical property is maintained, the kinds of greetings given to members and to nonmembers, the ways that funds are raised and disbursed, the architecture of the church (including the presence or absence of provision for the differently-abled), the parking facilities, the arrangement of the church office, the service and mission programs encouraged or discouraged, the newsletter, and the follow-up on visitors are all part of Christian education - intentionally or unintentionally.

While this book will focus primarily on those areas which are more traditionally considered Christian education, we should not forget the reality that the ministries and facilities of the church are continually teaching. We should ask of every activity and symbol of the church what is being taught about God, about Jesus Christ, about the responsibilities of Christians, about the view of visitors, and about the church's concern for the broader community and the world.

A Lack of Focus

Sadly some church growth efforts have failed to include sufficient focus on the ways in which the Christian education program affects the growth or decline of the congregation. This is especially ironic when many religious evangelists will readily admit that most of the persons who make confessions of faith during evangelistic meetings are persons who have had previous instruction in a local church (often during the elementary years).

Prominent church consultant Lyle Schaller, in his extremely helpful book *44 Ways to Expand the Teaching Ministry of Your Church*, writes that: "The teaching ministry often ranks second only to excellent preaching as a means of attracting new people to join the passing parade" [p.9]. Schaller further points out that the teaching ministry of the church is especially important when one hopes to see major growth among the generations born after 1945 [p.16].

The church growth movement has proven frustrating to many people because so much about the growth or decline of a particular congregation seems related to the demographic setting of the church. The local churches which have often been lifted up as the strongest examples of growing congregations are usually located in communities where the answer to these two questions is YES:

15

- Is the church in an area of high population growth?

- Is the church in an area which is popular with many young families?

When the answer to both questions is positive, the likelihood that the congregation will grow is much greater. Seminars, books, and denominational growth programs have often used those fast-growing churches as examples whose strategies should be followed in most other settings. The same strategies, however, do not produce the same results in settings which are characterized by population decline rather than growth.

The reality is that church growth is not easy to accomplish in our time. Even the churches located in areas of high growth will not increase membership without excellent preaching and excellent programming. Churches located in areas of declining population have a major task just keeping membership levels from declining at the same rate as the loss of people from the community.

While there are signs that the rate of decline in some mainline Protestant and Anabaptist churches may be slowing, the bottom line for most of those denominations has nevertheless been decline for many years. Although some evangelical denominations and parachurch organizations have experienced growth, that growth has very often been at a rate below the population growth.

Decline has certainly been evident in the Sunday school, with many denominations losing between a third and a half of their Sunday school attendance over the last twenty-five to thirty years. It is reasonable to believe that growth in Christian education, especially in the Sunday school, must receive major focus if the overall declines are to be reversed.

Catholic churches face many problems in financing, staffing, and recruiting students for parochial schools. Consolidations of Catholic elementary and secondary schools have become an apparent necessity in many parts of the country, but the loss of identity for the parishes involved often has significant negative consequences.

Some Christian educators have grown understandably uncomfortable with certain aspects of the church growth movement. While that movement correctly urges churches to focus more strongly on the needs of members and nonmembers, it is also true that an exclusive focus on church growth can result in the local church becoming yet another consumer seeking business and ignoring the peace and justice concerns which are also part of the gospel. Everything teaches something. An unhealthy focus on church growth can teach that peace and justice concerns are not important. The next chapter deals more with this issue.

Our motivation for reaching out through Christian education needs to be stronger than fear of not surviving as religious institutions, even though that fear is a rational one for some smaller denominations and local churches. The Bible in fact compels us to share the good news we have been given with others, to grow in discipleship, and to reach out to the needy of the world.

In *Rethinking Christian Education*, Richard Robert Osmer cautions that the basic question of a teaching church should not be "What must we do to survive?" but "What must we learn to find life?" When the church is no longer exclusively focused on growth or survival "based on the ability to meet people's needs, it is concerned with how it can best teach a pattern of truth and life that is faithful to the one who is the way, the truth, and the life" [p. 130]. Doing those tasks properly should result in a Christian education program which does intentionally reach out - not for the sake of survival as such but out of faithfulness to the gospel.

A False Tension:
Evangelism vs. Justice

> **Concept:** The need to reach out to those outside the faith through evangelism and the need to reach out to the poor and powerless through a passion for justice do not need to be in conflict. Both are responsibilities given to us by our Lord, and Christian education should embrace both needs.

When we started talking with people about a book with the title *Reaching Out Through Christian Education*, we received some responses we should have anticipated but in fact had not:

- "You're going to have to deal with liberals who'll see that title and think you're talking about working for peace and justice in the world. They won't understand that reaching out is about evangelism."

- "We don't need another book that tells people they should share the faith with others and work for church growth. Reaching out to the world should be about peace and justice - those are the concerns that have been too long ignored."

- "Churches have to make choices. Evangelical churches are geared for church growth, and that's what they do best. Mainline churches have tried too hard to grow and have failed to witness for peace and justice, which has traditionally been what set them apart."

- "If a church is really going to grow, then it has
  to focus on the needs of the people it wants
  to reach. You can't advocate social action
  strategies and have a church grow. If this book
  is going to be published by the Andrew Center,
  it had better be about church growth."

The reality is that a great many people involved in the life of the church feel that there is an inevitable tension between reaching out in evangelism and church growth activities and reaching out in peace and justice activities. The Bible, however, clearly tells us to do both. Two of the strongest admonitions of our Lord occur in the final chapters of the Gospel of Matthew - one commanding us to work for social justice and the other to share the faith with others:

- "For I was hungry and you gave me food, I was
  thirsty and you gave me something to drink,
  I was a stranger and you welcomed me, I was
  naked and you gave me clothing, I was sick
  and you took care of me, I was in prison and
  you visited me. . . . Truly I tell you, just as you
  did it to one of the least of these who are members
  of my family, you did it to me." [Matthew 25:35-36,
  40b]

- "Go therefore and make disciples of all nations,
  baptizing them in the name of the Father and of
  the Son and of the Holy Spirit, and teaching them
  to obey everything that I have commanded you."
  [Matthew 28:19-20]

The reality is that most people, in most of our churches, don't do a particularly great job of reaching out in either way. The Search Institute conducted a major study on effective Christian education and found that about two-thirds of the adults in our churches "have never or rarely encouraged someone to believe in Jesus Christ." Over half "have never given time to help the poor, hungry, or sick. With all the overt concern about youth, almost half of the adults report that they have never given time to help children, youth, or families." [David S. Schuller in *Rethinking Christian Education*, pp.6-7]

The scriptural emphasis on both forms of outreach suggests that our relationships with God are strongest when we embrace both approaches. That embracing needs to happen in the life of the church as a whole as well as in our individual lives.

Evangelism calls people to an intimate relationship with Jesus Christ, and those who grow in faith in that relationship should change in the ways that they relate to other people and to the needs of the world as a whole. In *Sharing Faith*, Thomas Groome urges that *"every aspect of the church's religious education curriculum, both its content and process, should be intentionally structured to form people's character in a faith that does justice for peace"* [p. 397, italics are his].

We may especially miss the mark when we fail to teach these concepts adequately starting with children. Dorothy Jean Furnish, in an essay titled "Rethinking Children's Ministry," reminds us that "children have an innate sense of justice - and outrage at the injustices in society" [In *Rethinking Christian Education*, p. 79]. They also have an innate desire to reach out in love to others and to share with others the things which excite or please them. They have certainly natural tendencies toward both social reform and evangelism - tendencies which all too often lose strength with the passage of time.

Another reality which we must face as we deal with these concerns is that our culture, both in the United States and in Canada, is increasingly pluralistic. Not all those around us are Christian, and not all those who are outside the Christian faith lack adherence to a belief system. The Jewish faith, Islam, Buddhism, Native American religions, and various New Age expressions of belief all have their followers.

Our concern for peace and justice needs to extend to all people, and our efforts at evangelism will not be effective if prefaced on the assumption that all who are not Christian are therefore nonbelievers. Christian education needs to help children, youth, and adults understand at least the basics of other faiths so that we can relate to those persons with respect. We will be far more successful at any efforts to win those persons to the Christian faith when we do not belittle what they already believe and when we support the full rights of all persons. [For a stimulating examination of this issue, read Martin E. Marty's "Christian Education in a Pluralistic Culture" in *Rethinking Christian Education*.]

Giving the specifics of full classroom content for any age level, of course, goes beyond the scope of *Reaching Out Through Christian Education*. That involves the curriculum which a church chooses to use and many other aspects of the church's teaching ministry.

Much of what is said in the first three parts of this book will be focused on organizing the educational ministry of the congregation in ways which involve more people in the educational programs and which bring unchurched people into a variety of "ports of entry." The assumption running through all these pages, however, is that a balanced program will include significant education about peace and justice issues and opportunities for that kind of outreach. The final part of this book deals with more specific examples of outreach based on the needs of particular groups of people.

What Is It Like
To Visit Your Church?

> **Concept:** First impressions do count! What is it like to visit your church?

The chapter titled "Everything Teaches Something" began with a summary of a visit to a local church in which the environment for an adult visitor was somewhat less than ideal. It's possible to get the same perspective on your own church without using the services of a consultant:

- Try looking at your own church as though you were a first time visitor. Think about how the various aspects of the church and its people would affect you. While it's impossible for any of us to be fully objective about our own congregations, you can still learn a great deal from this approach.

- Ask friends from another church or even from another community to visit your church in the role of volunteer consultants. Find out how they are welcomed (and not welcomed!) by others in the congregation. If the visit is to be effective, don't have them introduced to the congregation as your friends.

- Interview people who have recently visited your church. You want to seek out persons who have returned for additional visits and also

those who came one time and have not
returned.

No church looks the same to nonmembers as it does to
members. That discrepancy is greater in some situations than in
others. A consultant who visited a large downtown church on a
Sunday morning wrote these observations:

"One of the major difficulties facing this congregation is the
reality of two different views of the church. The first view is held
by those persons who are already active in the life of First
Church. Those persons are justifiably proud of the fine physical
facilities, the meaningful worship services, the excellent staff, the
large adult education program, and the fine lay leadership of the
congregation. They have also found deep and lasting friendships
and a sense of pride in the congregation.

"The second view is held by those who are chronically
inactive in the church and by those who only visit the church
one or two times. Those persons are uncertain where to park
their cars; have reservations about how safe the downtown area
near the church really is; do not know how to find the right
classrooms for themselves and members of their households; are
more critical of the appearance of the church school rooms; and
never stay long enough to feel accepted in a church school class.
Some of those persons even perceive the building and
membership as being snobbish."

In order to fully gain the second perspective, you need the
feedback of people who are not members of your congregation.
That's why having friends visit who are not known in the church
can be a valuable strategy. Similar insight may be available
through the feedback of recent visitors to your church, though
your friends may be more candid in what they share.

The following checklist may help you in thinking about the
impression your church makes on a first time visitor. While the
primary focus of this book is on Christian education, the list
includes several other items, both for your convenience in
evaluating the overall impact of your church on visitors, and
because all these factors work together to teach visitors whether
or not they are really welcome. Feel free to reproduce this
checklist for use in your church. [For another approach to
looking at your church, see the "Marketing Questionnaire" in
Steve Clapp's *Plain Talk About Church Growth*.]

How can visitors find out about your church?

_____ Is your church listed in the yellow pages?

_____ Are worship and Sunday school times included in the yellow page listing?

_____ If your summer schedule is different, does the yellow page listing give the summer schedule or suggest a call to the church office for the summer schedule?

_____ If you have child care available during worship and Sunday school for all ages, does the yellow page advertisement make that clear?

_____ If your church is accessible for the differently-abled, does that information appear in the yellow pages?

_____ Is there an answering machine on the church phone which provides information about the church's schedule?

_____ Is there a sign outside your church which is easy to read and which gives the correct times for worship and for Christian education?

_____ Do members of the congregation have a brochure, booklet, flier, or card that gives basic information about your church so that they can easily share that with people at work and in the neighborhood?

_____ If your church serves a particular "neighborhood," do you at least annually distribute information about the church in that neighborhood?

_____ If newspaper listings of church schedules are available without cost, do you take advantage of those listings? [If you must pay to be listed, then budget considerations and the circulation of the newspaper(s) become important factors. It is more important in most communities to be listed in the yellow pages than in a newspaper.]

Is your church easy to locate?

_____ Is the address clearly given in the yellow
pages, on printed materials of the church,
and on any message on the church's
answering machine?

_____ If your church is near but not on a major
street or route, is that information shared
to make it easier for people to find you?

_____ Do you have attractive, easy to read signs
on the streets approaching your church so
that it's easy for people to find?

What's it like to park near and to enter your church?

_____ Is church parking clearly marked?

_____ Are any spaces close to the building set aside
especially for visitors?

_____ If parking is permitted in a business lot near
your building, is there a prominent sign in
the church lot which explains where the
additional parking is available?

_____ Do you have "parking ushers" to greet people
as they arrive and direct them to parking
places? [Some churches have had exceptional
results with this and have found that the initial
greeting outside the church is appreciated by
visitors.]

_____ Is it easy for a visitor to determine which
entrance to the church should be used?

_____ If there are separate entrances for Christian
education rooms or the church office, are
those clearly marked?

_____ Are there greeters at the entrance(s) to your
church?

_____ Have the greeters been properly trained in how to extend warmth to visitors without being "pushy"?

_____ Do the greeters have basic information about the Christian education opportunities as well as worship services? [Do they know which adult classes are likely to be best for various ages and interests?]

_____ If your church is at all large, are maps which clearly mark classrooms displayed prominently around the building or given to visitors as they enter?

_____ Is there a brochure or flier which gives basic information about your church that can be handed to visitors?

_____ Do the greeters know the location of restrooms, child care, and coat racks?

The message of the facilities

_____ Are all the hallways clean and well maintained?

_____ Are there attractive bulletin boards in the church hallways?

_____ Are the restrooms clean and well maintained? (e.g., no peeling paint!)

_____ Are the classrooms attractive, clean, and well maintained?

Visitors to Christian education

_____ Are teachers prepared to greet new students as they enter the classroom?

_____ Are teachers of children comfortable introducing themselves to the parents of visitors? Do teachers

know whether or not visiting children should
remain in the room until their parents return?

_____ Are the rooms all neat, including updated
bulletin boards? [You may need to host an
occasional "Clean It Out Day" to dispose of old
materials and put up new ones.]

_____ Are class members encouraged to hang banners,
posters, and others results of class activity?

_____ Are teachers comfortable introducing visitors to
the rest of the class?

_____ Do teachers provide opportunity for some sharing
by class members to help visitors feel more at home?

_____ Is there a procedure to record the name, address,
and phone of any visitors to a class?

_____ Is there a procedure for sharing information about
class visitors with the church office?

_____ Do adult classes have coffee and tea available?

_____ Do youth classes have juice and donuts
available?

_____ Are extra copies of curriculum materials and other
study resources available for visitors?

_____ Are visitors informed of any coming social events
and encouraged to participate?

_____ Is there a procedure for follow-up on anyone
who visits a Christian education class or event?

_____ Do students in the class take a part in that follow-
up process rather than leaving it entirely to the
teacher or leader?

Visitors to worship

_____ Do greeters and ushers make it easy for visitors to get a bulletin and find a seat?

_____ Do you have a procedure for getting the names and addresses of visitors without putting them on the spot for a congregational introduction? [Approximately one-third of those who visit a church for the first time like being introduced to the entire congregation; two-thirds of first time visitors prefer greater anonymity.]

_____ Is the bulletin easy to follow for a visitor?

_____ Are there any major things which happen that are routinely not included in the bulletin?

_____ If the Lord's Prayer is included, does the bulletin indicate whether debtors, sinners, or trespassers is the word used? [That can simply be placed in parentheses after the title of the prayer.]

_____ Is the music well-performed and likely to be appealing to visitors?

_____ Are announcements done quickly enough that they will not be boring to visitors?

_____ Is there a children's sermon or another activity for children? [A short children's sermon can be valuable even if they are later dismissed for a children's church. A time for children says that they are important for the whole church.]

_____ Is the sermon skillfully delivered and interesting?

_____ Does the sermon give guidance for daily living?

_____ Does the sermon show a clear biblical base (which most people, including visitors, appreciate)?

_____ Is the sermon relatively brief? [15-20 minutes increasingly seems a good length relative to

the attention span of many people; a sermon
should be very good indeed to run as long as
30 minutes.]

[*If your church has an alternative or contemporary worship
service which uses drama, video, dance, or another approach
instead of a sermon, then the above questions need to be
modified.*]

_____ If communion [Eucharist, the Lord's Supper] is
served, are clear instructions given? Does the
bulletin or the pastor clearly state whether or
not nonmembers may share in communion?

_____ Is there a clear procedure to follow up on anyone
who visits a worship service?

_____ Are members of the congregation involved in that
follow-up process rather than leaving it all to staff?

The response of people to visitors

_____ Do people who do not have official responsibility
for visitors as greeters, ushers, or teachers take
the time to introduce themselves to visitors?

_____ Do the pastor and any other staff members take
the initiative to introduce themselves to visitors
and display warmth in that process?

_____ Is there a coffee and donut area where visitors
can mingle with church members before, between,
or after classes and services?

_____ Do members reach out to persons who are
standing alone during a coffee/fellowship time?

_____ Do visitors leave your church with an overall
impression that the congregation is open and
warm?

Evaluating and Dreaming

> **Concept:** Growing, improving Christian education programs take evaluation seriously and seek help in that process.

Those of us involved in most phases of the local church's program can easily find ourselves drifting from day to day and week to week. This can be especially true in a Sunday school or youth program, where the pressure of weekly preparation on the part of teachers, advisors, other volunteers, and staff makes it difficult to take an overall look at what is happening. On a given Sunday, we may recognize that we could be doing a better job; but we generally fail to act on that feeling as it fades in the pace of the new week.

The preceding chapter urged you to look at your church, especially the Christian education program, from the perspective of visitors. Now we want to examine that program from not only the perspective of visitors but that of leaders, students, and other concerned persons. The best overall evaluations generally come when we seek the input of many different persons. Take an overall look at your program by encouraging a large number of persons to complete a form like the one which follows. Compile the results and share them with the group responsible for Christian education (a board, commission, committee, or mission group depending on your local church structure) and with teachers and other leaders. In discussing the results, you'll identify specific changes which should be made. You have our permission to reproduce the form which follows for use in your church; modify the terminology as needed.

Christian Education Evaluation

Please help us evaluate the overall Christian education program of our church by completing this form. It is not necessary for you to put your name on the form, but we would appreciate your checking the background information requested in the first part of the evaluation. Your honest responses will be a significant help to our church.

Background information. Check the items which apply to you:

_____ Board/commission of education member
_____ Church school teacher
_____ Youth group advisor
_____ Sunday school class member
_____ Youth group member
_____ Small group member
_____ Church member for three years or more
_____ Church member for less than three years
_____ Not a member of the church
_____ Parent of a child
_____ Parent of a youth (junior or senior high)

How are we doing? Rate the job we seem to be doing in our Christian education program by using these symbols to respond to the items which follow:

E = excellent
G = good
OK = okay or satisfactory
P = poor
? = I don't have enough experience in this area to respond

_____ 1. The class I teach or attend does a good job holding the interest of those who come.
_____ 2. The class I teach or attend does a good job helping visitors and new members feel welcome.
_____ 3. If someone who has been regular stops attending the class I teach or attend, the class has a procedure to reach out to that person.
_____ 4. The class I teach or attend does a good job reaching out to persons who have become inactive in the church.
_____ 5. The class I teach or attend encourages members to reach out to unchurched friends, coworkers, and

31

neighbors.

___ 6. The class I teach or attend experiences a wide range of teaching methods.

___ 7. The class I teach or attend reaches out in service or mission to persons in need.

___ 8. The class I teach or attend responds to the needs and concerns of class members.

___ 9. The Sunday morning schedule isn't too crowded: there's sufficient time before classes for teachers to set up and after classes for teachers or class members to clean up and to talk with any visitors.

___ 10. Our church has available a good range of resource materials to help persons who teach (videos, books, etc.).

___ 11. Our church offers good orientation and training for those who teach.

___ 12. Our church recruits the best possible people to teach.

___ 13. Our church youth group does a good job holding the interest of those who attend.

___ 14. Our church youth group reaches out quickly to youth who stop attending.

___ 15. Our church youth group reaches out to youth who have become inactive.

___ 16. Our church youth group encourages group members to invite their unchurched friends.

___ 17. Our church youth group does meaningful service projects.

___ 18. Our church youth group helps visitors feel welcome.

___ 19. Our classrooms are in good repair.

___ 20. Our classrooms are consistently clean.

___ 21. Our classrooms are attractive and inviting.

___ 22. Our classrooms are clearly marked so visitors will have no difficulty knowing what class meets in a particular room.

___ 23. Greeters are available and do a good job helping people find the right class.

What should our priorities be? Using the scale provided below, indicate the extent to which more emphasis should be placed on the items which follow:

1 = A major priority
2 = More emphasis is needed, but this is not a major priority
3 = Present emphasis is reasonably adequate.

___ 24. Increasing membership and attendance at the children's level.

___ 25. Increasing membership and attendance at the youth level.

___ 26. Increasing membership and attendance at the adult level.

___ 27. Having videos and other media resources more readily available.

___ 28. Having craft materials more readily available.

___ 29. Recruiting additional teachers to make possible more team teaching.

___ 30. Providing better orientation and training for teachers.

___ 31. Recruiting additional youth group advisors.

___ 32. Providing better orientation and training for youth group advisors.

___ 33. Providing teachers and youth advisors with more opportunities to deepen their own spiritual lives.

___ 34. Providing more fellowship and sharing opportunities for teachers and youth advisors.

___ 35. Providing a wider range of study opportunities for adults in the church.

___ 36. Improving the physical appearance of our classrooms.

___ 37. Updating class lists so teachers and youth advisors know who *should* be in our classes and groups.

___ 38. Providing training to help our teachers and youth advisors know how to better reach out to the unchurched.

___ 39. Developing a better supply of substitute teachers.

___ 40. Finding ways to reach and serve the differently-abled (mentally and physically handicapped) through our education program.

___ 41. Providing support groups for persons who have gone through difficult times (such as the death of a loved one; divorce; alcoholism; ...).

___ 42. Providing spiritual life retreats for the whole church.

___ 43. Expanding opportunities for youth in the church.

___ 44. Developing children's program opportunities in addition to our present classes.

More sharing. Respond to the following items; feel free to use additional paper if needed:

45. What are the two best things which are currently happening

in the educational program at our church?

46. What are the two greatest needs in the educational program at our church?

47. If money, space, and volunteers were not barriers, what would your **dreams** be for our educational program?

48. If there is a particular dream which you have for our educational program that you would be willing to help become a reality, please indicate that dream and what you could do.

49. Please share the names of any persons you feel should be considered for leadership in our educational program along with a few lines about their skills.

50. Please feel free to add any other comments which would be helpful to us in evaluating our educational program.

Curriculum in a Media Dominated Age

> **Concept:** The cultural dynamics of our time make the challenge of selecting curriculum materials more difficult than ever. The primary criterion should be that curriculum materials used in your church are consistent with your faith tradition; then you can modify and supplement as needed.

Both the authors of this book have spent many years involved in the development, writing, and editing of curriculum materials. In fact it was while Jerry O. Cook was an editor of youth materials for the United Methodist Publishing House that he and Steve met each other. Steve, a local church pastor at the time, had written a letter to that organization which was critical of the youth curriculum, and the head of the department had invited him to complete a prospective writer's questionnaire. As Jerry was searching for new writers, he was intrigued by Steve's (slightly irreverently completed) questionnaire and letter of criticism.

Jerry invited Steve to come to the Publishing House for a conference and gave him a contract for a curriculum unit. That was the beginning of Steve's long career as a religious author and also the beginning of a long and strong friendship between Jerry and Steve.

The passage of time brought career changes for both of them, but they continued to be involved in curriculum development. Jerry left the Publishing House to pastor a local church and has written a large number of curriculum units from that perspective. Steve began devoting full-time to writing and consulting. During the same period of time Steve is working on this book, he is writing three units of youth curriculum for use in Anabaptist churches (Church of the Brethren, Brethren in Christ Church, General Conference Mennonite Church, and Mennonite Church).

Both of us have also developed and written curriculum materials for publishers who serve multi-denominational markets, and we've developed materials for children and adults as well as youth. Through the years, we have both had regular involvement teaching various age levels at the local church level and conducting workshops for others involved in teaching.

We share that information to help you understand the kinds of experiences we've had in working with curriculum materials. With each year that has passed, the curriculum production process has become increasingly difficult for almost every denomination for a variety of reasons:

- The production costs of curriculum materials have continued to rise, making it difficult to produce quality materials at prices local churches can afford.

- The attention span of children, youth, and (even) adults has definitely grown shorter with the impact of television and other media. Holding class interest demands a great variety in teaching methods and several changes in methodology within any given session.

- Because of the shorter attention span and the kinds of materials available in the secular world, curriculum materials have increasingly been evaluated on the basis of the amount of color and graphic attractiveness which are part of the publications. Those factors also raise production costs.

- With people across the United States having lower levels of loyalty to a particular denomination, it's not unusual for a class in a given local church to include persons from a wide range of backgrounds. Thus it becomes increasingly difficult in the preparation of materials for upper elementary, youth, and adult levels to assume any significant degree of prior exposure to traditional teachings

and beliefs of the denomination. Knowledge of
the Bible seems at an all time low, which presents
a great challenge to those who write curriculum
and those who teach.

• With many churches experiencing a shrinking
pool of volunteers and such a large percentage
of households having both parents working,
the average time available for preparation by
those volunteers who are teaching seems even
shorter than in the past. Curriculum materials
must address the challenge of using a wide
variety of methods to hold the interest of class
members while at the same time requiring as
little preparation time as possible.

Curriculum development and production has generally been
done for the entire United States, for all of Canada, or in some
cooperative efforts for both countries at the same time. It has
rarely been done on a regional level (Midwest, Southwest,
Northeast, Greater Chicago, etc.), and that has always presented
challenges. Steve Clapp is working on a curriculum unit while
living in Fort Wayne, Indiana; that unit will be used by teachers
in churches all across the United States and Canada including
inner city settings with mixed race congregations, large urban
churches, suburban churches, and small rural congregations.
Even with intentional field testing, it's sometimes difficult to
meet the needs of such diverse situations.

The preceding paragraphs may sound like rationalization for
some of the problems with curriculum materials. That's not our
intention! In fact we've both been critical of the curriculum
materials of our own traditions and from other sources. It is
important to recognize, however, that there are very real barriers
and limitations which the developers of curriculum must face.

Our own strong bias continues to be that the first choice in
curriculum materials, especially for children's classes, should be
from one's own denominational publisher. The reason for that
is simply that all curriculum materials offer a particular
theological point of view. If you use curriculum materials from
another denomination, then you are offering to your class the
theology of that denominational tradition rather than your own.
If you use materials from a so-called multi-denominational or
nondenominational publisher, you are still receiving the
theological perspective of that particular organization.

One large nondenominational publisher has over the years sold very impressive quantities of curriculum materials to churches of a specific denomination, and it just happens that the majority of that publisher's editorial positions are filled by persons from that denominational tradition! That's good for the particular denomination since so many of their churches use those materials, but it also means that perspective is the one which gets shared with persons from many other denominations who also buy from that publisher.

While there may be times that the materials from your own denomination are sufficiently weak that you have to look elsewhere, you do not want to take that step lightly. Without denominationally provided curriculum, it's very difficult to properly share teachings and traditions with children, youth, or adults.

As we look at reaching out to others, both on behalf of evangelism and on behalf of justice and peace concerns, it's important that we do our reaching out from the strength of understanding what we believe. While our individual beliefs are not always going to be consistent with denominational teachings, it's important for us to have been exposed to those teachings.

An alternative some churches use is that of developing their own curriculum materials or simply pulling ideas from a wide range of places. While that can be an attractive and exciting option if you have teachers willing to invest that amount of time and energy, there are also problems with this approach. First, the creativity of most of us is limited. When we are continually coming up with our own materials for classroom use, there's a natural tendency for us to frequently repeat the biblical passages, the issues, and the teaching methods with which we are personally most familiar and comfortable. Second, curriculum materials are generally developed so that over a two, three, or four year cycle, those who use the materials gain an overview of the major New Testament and Old Testament biblical passages. Important beliefs and traditions are covered in the same way. It's very difficult for any individual teacher to develop materials for classroom use which give that breadth of coverage over a period of time. Third, the time needed to develop a session from scratch each week is prohibitive for most people.

For all those reasons and more, we urge you to use the materials of your own denominational tradition when appropriate. That doesn't mean that you limit yourself to only the methods and approaches suggested in the curriculum materials. You may often want to broaden your range of activities; and the more comfortable you become with the teaching process, the easier it is to accomplish that. The next chapter gives a quick overview of a wide range of teaching methods.

If you do decide to use curriculum materials from a publisher other than your own denomination, then you should keep in mind several factors as you make decisions:

- Select materials from a publisher who seems
  reasonably compatible with your beliefs and
  traditions. Some are much better than others at
  this. In the opinion of one of this book's authors,
  Group (known especially for a multi-denominational
  youth magazine) has done a reasonably good
  job with the difficult task of supplying curriculum
  to churches of several different denominations
  without reflecting a theology which is too narrow
  or too superficial.

- Choose materials which are visually attractive,
  since these are more likely to hold the interest
  of students.

- Choose materials which use a wide range of
  methods and change methods frequently.

- Choose materials which encourage people to
  reach out to others both in evangelism and
  in justice and peacemaking activities.

Remember that whether you use denominational curriculum resources or those of another tradition, there will be times you will want to supplement those materials. For example:

- If you use materials from a nondenominational
  source, then you will need to add activities which
  teach your beliefs and traditions.

- You may want to experiment with the use of video
  to change the pace and hold the interest of
  students. That could mean selections from television
  programs and videocassettes of motion pictures
  (see the next chapter); the involvement of class

members in making their own video; or the use of videocassettes made especially for church use.

• Add artistic and craft activities to provide a greater diversity when appropriate.

• You will generally need to add service projects to help class members work with peace and justice issues.

• You will usually need to add activities and information which encourage class members to reach out to friends who are not connected with a local church.

• There will be events in the news which are relevant to what you are studying and which can provide the basis for meaningful discussions and activities. You will occasionally want to bring the newspaper into class.

Remember, finally, that curriculum materials do not teach. People teach. The gospel comes alive in the classroom because of the caring, the enthusiasm, and the commitment of those who teach. Curriculum is a tool, at its best an extremely valuable tool, but the teaching task is still performed by people. It's not enough just to provide good curriculum materials; we must also be prepared to give teachers the orientation and training they need to be effective. All of us who teach in the church need to cultivate our own spiritual lives, because the more depth we have ourselves, the more effectively we can lead others to deepened spiritual lives.

A Range of Methods

Concept: Teachers who use a variety of methods hold interest in their classes. Some methods may be especially helpful in attracting new class or group members.

Sunday schools have used a wide range of gimmicks to get students to classes including performances by strong men, talks by beauty queens, rides in hot air balloons, free goldfish, free bubble gum, free crosses, and a host of other enticements, surpassed only by McDonald's. A classic story involves a local church with a massive bus ministry. The story is true, but we'll leave out any identifying information in order to protect the guilty.

An eight-year-old girl was waiting outside her house for a ride to her Sunday school with some neighbors. While she was waiting, a bus from a church fifty miles away was driving through the subdivision to pick up students who were part of that church's extensive outreach. The driver mistakenly thought that the eight-year-old was on his passenger list. When he stopped for her, she gave him a puzzled look. "Aren't you going to Sunday school?" the driver asked.

"The Mitchells are going to pick me up in a few minutes."

"That's fine. Of course, you'll miss getting one of our goldfish."

"A goldfish?"

"This is free goldfish day. Everyone on the bus today gets a goldfish."

So the eight-year-old got on the bus. While she was on an eighty minute ride to the church and attending Sunday school and morning worship there, her neighbors and parents were frantic. The police were called, and a house to house search in the subdivision was begun. By the middle of the afternoon, the bus driver returned the girl, who, goldfish bowl in hand, asked her parents why there were so many police cars on the street.

That's the extreme. It's hard to say precisely where the line should be drawn on promotional strategies for Christian education, but we'll argue giving away goldfish and picking up children who live fifty miles away are both going too far.

Our focus here is not primarily on methods or gimmicks to get children to come but on a variety of methods for use in the classroom once they've arrived. Classes which are well conducted utilizing a variety of methods, however, create a setting to which children and young people especially want to invite their friends.

This is not a book on teaching methods. Excellent publications, which give a broader range of teaching/learning strategies, are available from both secular and religious sources. The arrangement of methods we're presenting here is intended as a quick guide to help you when you want activities to supplement curriculum plans or to use in presenting topics which come without study guides.

Artistic expression and crafts: Most children and young people enjoy creative activities. Some people who cannot express themselves well in words may find special meaning in work with clay, block prints, painting, banners, collage making, and so forth. As school systems in many parts of the country continue to cut back on instructors and materials for art classes, opportunities for creative expression in the church gain in appeal. Artistic expression can be a valuable teaching method, and special interest groups in creative expression may be a draw for some children and young people.

Remember that the possibilities are enormous:
- cartoons
- doll making
- drawing
- finger painting
- sculptures
- write-on or photo slides
- wire sculptures

Many churches find that they can facilitate artistic expression and craft activities by having a central supply room which is well stocked with needed materials so that teachers normally count on finding what they need without going shopping each week. Some churches maintain supply cabinets or closets in each classroom and have a volunteer who keeps them stocked so that the teaching teams do not have to do so.

While we think of these activities as being especially for children and youth, you might be pleasantly surprised at how well some adult classes will respond to the opportunity to express themselves in a nonverbal manner.

Music: Music is an integral part of life for children and young people. Popular songs on radio and MTV make strong impressions on them. If you work with youth, then you should make an effort to be aware of what teenagers are listening to in your community and encourage the young people with whom you work to talk about that music. Some popular music does convey values which are inconsistent with the Christian faith, but it's better to help young people to critically evaluate that music than to simply complain at them for listening to it.

There are also a growing number of Christian artists whose work has begun to be successful even in secular arenas. Amy Grant has experienced considerable commercial success and still takes seriously her responsibilities as a Christian. Be careful, however, about automatically assuming it is better for children and youth to listen to popular Christian music than to popular secular music. Some popular Christian music conveys values which may not be consistent with your denominational teachings and traditions.

Most children's curriculum contains a variety of songs for classroom use. Take advantage of these whenever possible. Keyboards, guitars, and autoharps are especially good for accompaniment in the classroom setting.

Children's choirs can be a valuable addition to corporate worship, and the opportunity to sing in a choir may be a significant draw to unchurched children in some parts of the country where there are few musical opportunities in the public schools.

Video: Video provides some fascinating opportunities for classroom use. Some companies, like the Paulist Fathers, Word, Focus on the Family, and Ecu-Film, offer videos made especially for church use. You may also find that showing brief segments from television shows and secular videos can stimulate interesting discussion. For example:

- Show the graveside scene from *Steel Magnolias* in which the friends of the grieving mother (who is played by Sally Field) attempt in their own awkward way to comfort her after the committal service for her daughter. The scene raises questions about the meaning of friendship, theological issues about life and death, and the matter of how to reach out to persons who are in pain.

- Show the scene from *Grand Canyon* in which the black tow truck driver saves a white man who is in danger from a young gang. The scene raises questions about black and white relationships, poverty and crime, and grace and courage. It could also be an interesting beginning to a discussion about the contemporary meaning of the story of the Good Samaritan.

The preceding clips are for youth and adult use, not for children's classes. Video clips from movies like *Aladdin* and *Homeward Bound* can work well with children.

Also remember the possibility of making your own videos as a class or group. Increasing numbers of churches have video cameras, and there are generally several congregational members who have that equipment. A modern telling of some of the parables of Jesus could make a fascinating class project for many different age levels. Also consider making videos to give a Christian perspective on issues like drugs, crime, poverty, health care, and sexuality. Those kinds of activities require a great deal of work but also have the power to draw new people to the class or group.

Drama: Drama in many forms can give creative outlets to persons of all ages. Puppet shows, ventriloquism performances, role plays, mini-dramas, dramas, shadow plays, and pageants can be powerful tools for classroom learning and for sharing the gospel. Consider these possibilities:

- Have a drama group for youth which produces one or two plays a year. These groups can be an excellent way to draw youth who are not interested in more traditional church activities.

- Develop a puppet show or a ventriloquism show which

44

can be used to enrich Sunday school classes and also for performances at shopping malls, community organizations, hospitals, and nursing homes.

• Help students in classes make their own puppets to use in telling Bible stories. Use them in the classroom, have programs for parents, and arrange community performances.

• Form an adult dramatic group or reader's theater. Do two or three performances a year which can be shared in morning worship and then taken to other church and community organizations.

• Form a special summer theater group at the church. Involve adults and young people. Go "all out" on publicity, and pack the church basement or fellowship hall for "Theater in the Round." Consider the possibility of making this a dinner theater.

• Class members and teachers can develop skill in storytelling - both biblical stories and their own stories.

You can make drama easier at the classroom level by keeping a box filled with costumes and props in a central area or in each room. You can get families to donate old clothes, masks, canes, and other supplies.

Clown ministries: Clowning gives many people a new freedom to share their faith and their concern for others. Many people can be less self-conscious as a clown and thus find it easier to reach out to others. Ask one or two people in your church to gain skill in clowning and then utilize them to help various classes and groups experiment with this medium. Also consider:

• Having a "Clown Camp" as part of your Vacation Bible School.

• Use clowns to promote special events at the church. They can make the rounds of shopping malls, streets, homes, and businesses. Many people who would be reluctant to invite others to church under normal circumstances find it much easier to be outgoing as a clown.

• Have a special group of youth who specialize in clowning. Such efforts often have special appeal to inactive and nonmember young people. The group can do clowning in hospitals, nursing homes, and shopping centers.

Always be sure to obtain permission before doing clowning in a nursing home, hospital, or shopping center.

Bubbles: Bubbles have excellent potential as settings for Christian education and as a means of outreach. A bubble is simply a big, inflated plastic meeting area. You can talk inside a bubble; write on the walls of a bubble; and show slides or films on the sides of a bubble. Students enjoy making them, and they are relatively inexpensive. You can use them as a setting for class discussions; as an interest spot for church festivals and family suppers; and as an attention-getter on the church lawn or at a shopping mall. Consider setting up a bubble at a shopping center and using it as a place to display information about world hunger. Making a bubble is easy:

1. Use plastic drop cloths for the bubble. These are inexpensive to purchase from most paint or hardware stores. Don't buy the cheapest you can find - spend an extra thirty cents a drop cloth to get thicker plastic.

2. Electrical tape can be used to fasten together the edges of several drop cloths. You want to leave room for a fan to be attached at one end and for an entrance flap at the other end. There needs to be enough overlap [at the point of the entrance flap] to permit people to enter and leave the bubble without deflating it.

3. A fan taped securely at one end of the bubble provides the air to inflate it. Do not, of course, leave the fan running unless supervised by an adult.

4. Bubbles work fine outdoors - unless there is a big wind! You can easily run an extension cord for the fan.

5. People obviously need to be careful about poking holes in the bubble, but you can normally write on it easily with markers.

If you've not made a bubble before, it's generally best to try it yourself before attempting it with a group. They are easy to make, but practice helps!

Writing: Writing activities can also be valuable creative outlets. Have class or group members write their own scripts for a drama or a video. Have people write letters to shut-ins, prison inmates, or people in the armed forces. Have people write devotionals and prayers (and consider using those to make your own class devotional booklet during the Easter or Christmas seasons). Litanies, poetry, and stories can all be valuable experiences.

Guests: Have guests come to your class to share experiences or information which will be helpful. Possibilities:

• The minister to talk about baptism or communion.

• A physician to give information on maintaining the body as a temple of God or to talk about ethical issues in medical practice.

• A rabbi to give perspective on the Jewish faith.

• Parents for a session on family life.

• Members of another class for a shared study or program.

• A social worker to give information on local hunger needs.

• A class from another church which includes people of different races than those in your church.

• Grandparents (or "grand persons" for those who do not have grandparents living close enough to come).

• A missionary to give perspective on the church's outreach.

Another strategy can be having members of your class or group use tape recorders to interview people in the community and then share those with the class.

Travel: Travel can be a valuable means of relating the Christian faith to daily life. Travel programs seem especially helpful in trying to reach teens who are not interested in traditional church activities and when trying to reach young adults. Consider:

- A trip to mission sites of your denomination.

- A trip to Washington D.C. to the Holocaust Museum.

- A trip to the Holy Land for adults or families.

- Weekend camping getaways for church members who enjoy tent and trailer travel. Instead of seeing their travel as competitive with Sunday worship and classes, arrange outings for them - and provide worship and study as part of the weekend.

- Exchange programs between churches which serve different settings: urban and rural; black and white. Have the ministers swap pulpits, and have some members travel along.

- Taking your class or group to a hospital, a nursing home, or a jail to visit with those who are living in such settings. Depending on the distance involved, you may be able to do this during a Sunday morning class. (Of course you need to make arrangements in advance.)

Self-Directed Learning: Some churches are experimenting with self-directed learning. This can involve a range of activities carried out by individuals rather than by groups. Examples include: doing Bible study with the guidance of a workbook; listening to audio tapes; watching videos; sharing with people in other locations through satellite television connections; and completing exercises on computer. Obviously these kinds of experiences do not provide the kind of group interaction which we normally expect in Christian education. As Sara R. Little has pointed out in an essay in *Rethinking Christian Education*, "the general adult education literature is too pervasively inclusive of such ideas to ignore them" [p.108]. These methods may provide helpful flexibility for persons whose schedules do not permit involvement in regular classes and an interesting change of pace for others.

Part Two:

Reaching Out
Through Leadership

*Then he said to his disciples,
"The harvest is plentiful, but
the laborers are few; therefore
ask the Lord of the harvest to
send out laborers into his
harvest."*

Matthew 9:37-38

Add Leaders Before Adding Students

> **CONCEPT:** Local church educational programs often fail to grow because they are understaffed. An insufficient number of teachers can cause decline in attendance. Adding teachers and other leaders almost always makes it easier to add students.

When a church wants to grow through its educational ministry, it seems logical to find creative ways to add students and then to add teachers as needed. It may be logical, but it generally doesn't work. Consider these facts:

• Recruiting efforts only succeed in getting people to a class or group one time. The skill, concern, and commitment of the teacher or teachers determine whether or not new students return.

• New children and youth need to form a solid identity not only with the other students but also with adult leadership. In fact, most new students find it easiest to identify with a teacher first and then later with class members. A single teacher confronted with more than one or two new students at a time may find it difficult to build the kind of bond which is important.

• Prompt follow-up on students who break patterns of attendance is crucial to conserving present students and to ensuring the continuation of new students. That job is best done by the teacher(s), but it is more likely to be done if the time required is not too great for any one person.

• The rolls of most local churches include the names of many children, young people, and adults who were active at one time, but who no longer attend. This can be an extremely fertile area of evangelism if there is adequate volunteer time to follow up on these persons. Studies continue to show that children and youth who have become inactive are much easier to bring back to involvement than are adults who have become inactive; children and youth do not feel the same need to explain their absence that adults often do and thus can respond more readily to invitations to return.

• Such rolls are in existence only because people of previous years spent the time to maintain the records. It's likewise important that current records of Sunday school and C.C.D. attendance be well maintained. Again, this is a much easier job if the class has more than one teacher.

Many Sunday school classes experience a **growth limit** based on the number of teachers or leaders. For very young ages, each adult teacher or leader should not be responsible for more than four children. Even at the upper elementary and youth levels, it's unrealistic to expect classes to go smoothly if a single teacher or leader is responsible for more than eight students.

A team of two persons for a class may place a limit of sixteen on the growth potential for that group because of the natural tendency of such classes to level out at that ratio. The growth limit will be lower if one of the teachers is frequently absent. Teachers communicate the love of Christ to class members, and one person can only do that successfully with a few others at a time. The fact that public school classes have twenty, thirty, or even more students in one room with one teacher has almost nothing to do with Christian education settings, which are based on volunteer teachers and students.

Plan for growth in your Sunday school, C.C.D. class, or other groups by recruiting an adequate number of teachers and other leaders. Team teaching (two or more persons working with the same class or group) is the most effective approach with classes and groups of children and youth. It makes it possible for people to share, not only the actual teaching responsibility, but also a number of tasks which can help the class grow, including follow-up on visitors, follow-up on persons who stop attending, and special efforts to get other persons to attend.

Team teaching also makes it easier for leaders to miss a Sunday of attendance without harming the continuity of the class.

While team teaching may be the ideal, persons who are not interested in teaching can still make valuable contributions to a class or group. A person might be assigned to a class, for example, just for the purpose of implementing strategies to encourage growth. Some people like working with crafts or music, but are not comfortable with other tasks that are normally part of the teaching process.

The following steps can be very helpful, especially if begun before the start of the educational year:

1. Recruit enough teachers and leaders to have at least two for each class or group. If classes or groups already have more than twelve active students, recruit enough people to have a ratio of one teacher or leader to every six active students at the children and youth levels (one to every three toddlers). Those ratios give you room for growth. At the adult level, one teacher or leader may be sufficient for fifteen to twenty class members, but you'll still find it easier to focus on growth when more persons have accepted leadership responsibility.

2. Be sure that the rolls of names, addresses, and phone numbers of classes are updated.

3. Establish a committee or task force for each class or group which is given the goal of adding members to the class. That committee should take the class roll and should also brainstorm for the names of prospective students who have never been active in the church. Children and youth can think about people in their neighborhood and from school. Adults can think about work associates and neighborhood residents. You may be surprised at the number of names which you can generate of persons who are not currently involved. The committee can be composed of class members or parents and the teachers.

4. The teachers and the committee should carry out a concentrated effort at contacting each prospective student - ideally with a home visit and certainly with a telephone call.

5. If necessary, transportation should be arranged for new students the first couple of Sundays at least. Even if they have

transportation of their own, people are far more likely to attend if picked up.

6. When new students arrive for class or group activities, the teacher should take the initiative in sharing their names with the class and in helping people become better acquainted.

7. The week following the first attendance at a class, the teacher should:

- Write or call to share appreciation for that person's attendance.

- Notify the pastor of the call having been made.

- Arrange for another student to call the newcomer and extend an invitation to share a soft drink or some other social event during the week. Coffee or tea for adults!

8. Be prepared to follow up the first time there is a break in the attendance pattern of any new or continuing student.

Recruiting Teachers and Group Leaders

CONCEPT: Most churches do have an adequate supply of persons who can be effective teachers and group leaders, but recruitment must be done with care.

A church's educational program will not grow in quality or quantity without dedicated, caring teachers and leaders. There is no point mounting an elaborate publicity program or neighborhood canvass unless classes and groups are adequately staffed with people who:

1. Care about others and can demonstrate Christ's love through their relationships.

2. Care about teaching and are willing to do the necessary preparation.

3. Are loyal to the beliefs and practices of your denomination, so they will not work against the rest of your church's program.

4. Recognize the importance of keeping records that enable follow-up on those who become inactive.

5. Are willing to pray for and visit with persons who have become inactive.

6. See outreach to others as an integral part of
the Christian faith and will encourage class
or group members to do the same.

There is a natural institutional tendency for churches to "cream off" what is considered the best lay leadership for positions such as trustees, board of deacons, finance, parish council, governing board, pastoral relations committee, and so forth. That trend can be a costly one.

It is vitally important that being a teacher or group leader in a church is viewed by the staff and congregation as a position of great importance. You need people of the highest possible quality in those positions.

Although there are various ways of dealing with this matter, one extremely effective one is to have a single nominating committee identify persons for all the leadership positions in the church. Many local churches have a nominating committee which takes care of all positions except those in the educational area; educational positions are filled by the efforts of the education commission or whatever group is responsible for that program. Thus those groups become competitors for the talent of the church. A single group charged with the responsibility of recruiting for the needs of the church will do a better job sorting through the available talent and using people where they will be most effective.

Some churches have had great success using a spiritual gifts discernment program which helps people identify their own talents and interests and then attempts to match them with the needs of the church. The *Networking* program written by Bruce Bugbee and published by Zondervan is especially excellent. Other high-quality spiritual-gift-based programs are available through the Church Growth Institute, the Fuller Institute, and Net Results.

The minister plays a crucial role in determining the priority which is given to recruitment of top quality people for work in education. If the minister clearly feels education is a priority, then that attitude will be picked up by the group responsible for nominations and by others in the church.

The following suggestions about recruitment grow out of discussions with churches from twenty-two different denominations. They also reflect comments made on a survey completed by persons who were not involved in an educational program at that time. If you use a spiritual gifts discernment program, some of these suggestions will not be relevant, but most will be.

56

1. Never assume that someone is unwilling to teach. Phrases like these are frequently heard in nominating meetings:

- "He tried teaching third graders once and just hated it. We shouldn't ask him again."

- "Oh, no. She won't teach a class. I know that."

- "She teaches all day. She wouldn't want to teach a group in the evening or on Sunday."

- "He's always been church treasurer. We can't ask him to do anything else."

In each instance, the speaker is assuming that the person will not want to teach a class. While that assumption may be correct, it is not always correct.

The first question for a nominating meeting should not be: "Would this person be willing to be a teacher?" The better question to consider is: "Would this person be a good teacher, and is that the best place to use this person's skills and gifts?" If the answer to the question is YES, then let the individual being considered decide whether or not to teach.

In *Christian Education in the Small Church*, Donald Griggs and Judy McKay Walther suggest that it may be better to speak of "inviting" than of "recruiting." "The process of recruiting seems to imply pressure and hard sell" [p. 54]. We can't avoid some use of the word recruiting in talking about the process, but the concept of invitation is a more positive one to use in approaching people. We are *inviting* people to be part of an exciting, rewarding ministry, and we should convey to them that it is an honor to be asked to teach in the church.

2. Offer training or orientation for new teachers and leaders. If your church is small, this may be very informal. It could involve a past teacher or advisor, the minister, and a member of the class or group sitting down with the new teacher or teachers and reviewing what has been done in the past, sharing possibilities for the future, and going over curriculum and other resources. The next section discusses other approaches to training which you'll want to consider.

People often do not volunteer because they genuinely feel inadequate. The knowledge that they will be given resources and backing is extremely helpful.

3. With youth and adult classes, involve class members themselves in the recruiting or inviting process. Have the class or group brainstorm the names of persons whom they would enjoy as leaders. When the appropriate nominating group has made a selection, ask one or more class members to share in extending the invitation.

This procedure is especially effective in recruitment for youth classes and groups. Many potential adult leaders are somewhat intimidated or threatened by a room full of junior highs or senior highs. The knowledge that the class or group itself wanted that person as a leader is very reassuring. Further, it is much harder to turn down a teaching invitation when a young person is part of the team that extends the invitation.

4. Don't recruit by letter or phone! Instead make an appointment for a visit at the convenience of the prospective volunteer. A 1993 study of local church recruiting efforts showed the following range of positive responses (by percentage) on the basis of the manner in which the approach was made:

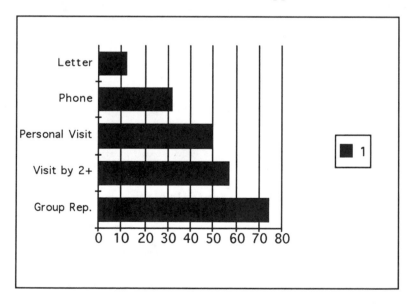

As the chart shows, letters and phone calls were far less effective at obtaining positive responses than the other three strategies, which all centered around visits in the home or at lunch. The visit being made by one person resulted in a positive response 49% of the time. The acceptance rate rose to 57% when the visit was made by two or three persons, and it rose to 74% when one of those persons was a representative of the class or group.

Making individual appointments and using teams for recruitment may seem cumbersome, but it can also save time in the long run. If you genuinely go after your best, most talented prospects, your odds of the invitation being accepted are very high. Let the person know this is an important position and that he or she is the best person available. Persons who are recruited in this manner are also more likely to continue teaching for several years.

Some churches may face the problem that the number of persons involved in the nominating process is not sufficient for all recruitment to be done using personal visits and teams. If you use other strategies, at least do so aware that your acceptance rates will not be as high; consider team visits for the positions that it will be most difficult to fill.

Do be careful not to use the team recruitment model to badger or harass the prospective volunteer into accepting the invitation. Persuasion is one thing; dumping guilt is another. Persons who are coerced into a position do not stay long!

5. Recruit both men and women! Although much of secular society continues to be dominated by men rather than by women, the realm of Christian education was for many years largely one of female domain at the local church level. That situation has been changing with very positive results. Men have a great deal to contribute to Christian education, and increasing numbers of churches are using men, not only for youth and adult classes, but also for work with children. Consider:

- having husband and wife teaching teams.

- inviting men to be the monitors for classes which have proven difficult to control.

- having a special recruitment thrust emphasizing the need for male teachers.

- using men to teach some of the preschool classes. As there are increasing numbers of single parent homes, the majority of which are headed by women, small children very much need contact with adult males as well as with adult females.

6. Recruit an adequate number of teachers. Nothing burns out volunteers faster or frightens potential volunteers away more quickly than having too little adult help. Discipline problems, headaches, and preparation time decrease when classes and groups are adequately staffed. Ideally you should have a teacher or adult counselor for every six children or youth in a class. Under no circumstances should you have a ratio of more than ten children or youth to an adult teacher or advisor. A person who is currently teaching alone can be very effective in helping recruit one or two additional persons to make a team teaching situation possible. The same study referred to in suggestion five also showed that persons were significantly more likely to agree to accept a team teaching position than the full, individual responsibility for a class or group.

7. Recruit teachers for a set period of time, and then let them renew the arrangement if they wish. A year is usually a good length of time, though most will want to continue for more than a single year.

A caution is appropriate: too many churches have become dependent on systems in which teachers are rotated with great frequency. For example, a person may only be asked to teach every other quarter or even just a single quarter during the year. This procedure is attractive from the standpoint of some potential teachers, but it can be disastrous for a class. Students need the continuity of regular teachers in the classroom. This is especially important for infant, nursery, and kindergarten classes. Small children cannot understand changes in leadership, and those changes are not fair to the children. Parents want the security of knowing the people who take care of their children during the educational time.

Elementary children and youth need the freedom to share problems, fears, and anxieties within church classes and groups. They will not feel that freedom if leadership changes rapidly. Team teaching can provide greater flexibility for teachers while guaranteeing that one or two people who are familiar will be present each week. Adult classes can generally work with considerably more autonomy in recruiting their own leadership, and rotating leadership may not work badly. The situation with children and youth is not the same.

Rotating leadership, however, is not good in a new adult class. At the beginning of a new adult class, the responsibilities on the teacher for the establishment of continuity and tradition are considerably greater than in an adult class which has had a long history. There is some evidence that new classes are most successful when the same teacher continues for a period of at least three years.

8. Consider a system of a "teacher in preparation" or a "counselor in preparation." Recruit an individual or a couple several months or even a year in advance. Have them share in group or class activities without having to take major leadership responsibilities. They will have established good relationships with class members before accepting the full responsibility for the group.

9. Consider having an annual supper or workshop (or workday) to which both present and potential teachers are invited. Make it clear in the invitation to potential teachers that attendance at the workshop does not place them under obligation to teach. An orientation to materials and methods often helps people feel more comfortable about the invitation to teach.

10. Provide sufficient support to teachers and leaders so that they are enabled to feel good about themselves and about their work. More ideas for this are shared in the next section.

Teacher Training, Support And Reinforcement

Concept: Teachers and other education leaders who have been well-trained and who are supported and encouraged will be far happier with their work and will do a more effective job reaching others for Christ.

"I'd quit teaching Sunday school, but I know they can't find anyone else." "I wish I could quit helping with C.C.D., but our priest really needs the help." "When you agree to teach in this church, you've made a lifetime commitment." Those statements come from people who feel "trapped" into continuing to teach in the church. Such comments should be taken seriously. Some of us like to complain and will complain about anything - no matter how well life is going. But persons who genuinely feel taken advantage of or who are just plain tired of teaching for so long need to be given a rest.

Part of what makes many teachers respond that way, however, is the reality that they've received relatively little training, support, or encouragement from the church. While any of us can grow weary of a particular volunteer job and crave a change of pace, people continue far longer and give far superior performance when they're properly trained for the responsibilities they're given and when they receive continuing support and encouragement in their work. All of us want to know that our efforts are making a difference, and we also want to know that our efforts are appreciated.

Teachers are the center of any strong Christian education program. Your educational program will not grow unless teachers are enthusiastic about what is happening. Thus the preparation of teachers and their reinforcement become of great importance. Consider these ideas:

1. Always provide orientation for new teachers and leaders. As discussed in an earlier section, the orientation can be very informal in nature. It may involve a past teacher, the minister or another staff member, and a member of the class or group. If someone is becoming a new member of a teaching team, the other person or persons on that team can take care of the orientation. Orientation should cover points such as the following:

- What the goals and philosophy are of the Christian education program in your church. Be sure that new teachers and leaders understand what your church wants to accomplish through Christian education and how Christian education relates to the overall life of the church.

- How to effectively use the curriculum.

- What help is available with crafts, music, and media.

- Where and how to obtain craft, music, and media materials.

- The significant characteristics and needs of the age group or the interest focus of the class or group.

- Background about the nature of the class or group. What methods have been well received in the past? What problems have occurred in the life of the group?

- How to obtain reimbursement for expenses.

- The procedures used in maintaining attendance records and in following up on persons who are absent.

- How to reach out to involve new people in the class or group, and what reporting should be done to the pastor or others when visitors attend the class or group.

- When important special events, meetings, and emphases will take place. When are teacher meetings and training events scheduled? Is there a special Christmas program in which all classes participate? Is there a special Lenten emphasis? People need these dates well in advance. Ideally the calendar for the whole program year should be shared at least a couple of months before that year begins. If your program year starts in September, have the important dates available at least by July.

- What service projects to families, others in the church, the community, and the world have been done in the past or are possibilities for the future.

- What procedures should be followed when the teacher or leader must be absent.

- Who should be contacted if the teacher or leader needs help or support with a student in the class, with a problem being encountered, or with a service opportunity which should be pursued.

- Opportunity to discuss other questions and concerns of the new teacher or leader.

Some of these matters will be common to most classes or groups and can perhaps be covered in a teachers' meeting or training session for a number of people at the same time. That kind of event, however, doesn't replace the need for orientation to be provided on a personal basis, focused just on the particular class or age group involved.

2. Plan at least two teacher training/enrichment/ workshop days during the school year. These may be events sponsored just by your local church, events offered by your denomination, or events sponsored by a local ministerial association or other ecumenical organization. These provide teachers with more ideas and also with new bursts of enthusiasm and energy. Possible topics include:

- How to more effectively help class members share their faith with friends.

- How to more effectively use storytelling in the class or group.

- Ideas for new craft activities.

- Ideas and strategies for service projects.

- How to creatively use media in the classroom.

- How to help children and youth produce their own videos.

- Introduction to a wide range of methods for class and group use.

- How to more effectively use drama and role playing in the classroom.

- How to teach listening and caring skills so that class or group members can more effectively respond to one another, to family and friends, and to persons in special need of caring.

- Ways to involve the families of children and youth in class activities.

- How to effectively handle behavior problems.

- How to more effectively plan and evaluate class or group sessions.

- Strategies for enhancing the self-esteem of class or group members.

Demonstration classes or laboratory schools offer an especially valuable strategy for improving the skills of teachers. In a demonstration class, teachers of a specific age level class or group get to observe a very experienced teacher instruct students of the same age level. This lets them learn first hand new ways to present materials and interact with students. A laboratory school is similar, but generally lasts longer and gives opportunity for the persons being trained to actively participate in leadership in addition to observing. Because of the number of different age level classes involved, these experiences often must be offered on a denominational or community-wide basis. Most local churches do not have enough teachers to be trained to justify separate demonstration or lab classes for: nursery, kindergarten, elementary 1-2, elementary 3-4, elementary 5-6, junior high, senior high, and adult. It usually takes the cooperative efforts of several churches to successfully sponsor these events.

3. Have an open house or party for teachers and other educational leaders. This kind of event is an affirmation of the contribution teachers are making, a time of good companionship, and also an opportunity for people to share the hopes and frustrations they may be experiencing in the teaching process.

4. Have a system of age level directors or counseling teachers. You might have a children's director, a youth director, and an adult director. If your church is larger, then a system of counseling teachers may be more effective, with a counseling teacher available for each age level (nursery, kindergarten, etc.). The director or counseling teacher should periodically check with teachers to find out their needs and concerns. When possible, the director or counseling teacher responds immediately to the need with information, resources, or the arrangement of a conversation with another person. The director or counseling teacher should ideally have had successful experience teaching the particular age level so that he or she readily understands the frustrations and opportunities of that work.

The age level directors or counseling teachers also provide a valuable service in linking the needs of classroom teachers with the education commission or other group which has the basic responsibility for Christian education in the church. The director or counseling teacher interprets attendance goals, Christmas play plans, and other overall emphases to classroom teachers. That person also sees that problems teachers are experiencing get communicated to the education commission.

5. Have a special recognition of teachers and other educational workers at a morning worship service at the start and/or the end of the educational year. This reinforces the worth of those persons and keeps the congregation aware of the importance of educational programming. Some churches have a dedication or consecration of teachers in the fall, when most Christian education program years begin, and then a service of appreciation in the spring or summer. It's good to give a book or another small gift at the time of the recognition, and many churches combine the worship recognition with a breakfast, brunch, or dinner that honors educational workers.

6. Remember that sincere, informal recognition means a great deal to volunteers. Formal services of recognition and gifts are important and should be part of the church's program, but they are not always as meaningful as some more informal communications. Education commission members, age level directors or counseling teachers, and church staff members can provide valuable reinforcement to teachers by:

- Writing a short note to a teacher to share that a class member was heard talking about how great the class is.

- Calling a teacher on the phone to share that a new member is being received into the church because of the efforts of that teacher.

- Stopping by the classroom at the end of a class or group to ask how things are going and to share appreciation for the teacher's continued work.

- Clipping or photocopying an article from a newspaper, magazine, or journal which might be of help to the teacher and sending it along with a note of thanks for that person's continued work.

7. Class members and the parents of children can do a great deal to reinforce the work of teachers. Affirmation means most when it comes directly from class members or from parents who relay children's reactions to class experiences. Urge class members and parents to use strategies such as the following to share appreciation with teachers:

- Class members who clearly prepare ahead of time reinforce the importance of the class to them and at the same time are sharing with the teacher the affirmation that "this class is a vital part of my life." This especially applies to adult classes.

- Urge class members or parents who have shared appreciation for a teacher to personally write a note or make a phone call to that teacher.

- Teachers like to assume, hope, and know that someone somewhere prays for their teaching efforts, strength, and wisdom. Class members and parents can let teachers know of their prayers.

There is also a sense in which affirmation is shared when a class member or a parent takes the time to share a criticism or a suggestion with a teacher. That doesn't mean criticism feels good at the moment it is received, but most people recognize that it comes out of respect for the individual and appreciation for the importance of the teaching task. It might be compared to the perspective of a chef in a good restaurant: "If quality is lacking, tell *me*. If it's good, tell me and your friends."

8. The provision of a Christian education handbook for your church can be of great value to teachers and other leaders. A handbook usually shares the goals, philosophy, job descriptions, procedures, and any other information which will be helpful to teachers and other educational workers. Goals and philosophical issues were discussed earlier in this book, and a future section gives sample job descriptions.

9. Be sure that craft and art materials, books, and media resources are readily available to teachers. Even relatively small churches find it useful to have a person who accepts the responsibility of keeping craft and artistic expression materials on hand. This may be through a central storage room or closet for all classes or through regular checking and restocking of materials in each classroom. Markers, crayons, finger paints, glue, tape, scissors, paper, newsprint, posterboard, and other materials can be purchased with less expense and effort when one person does it on behalf of the church. If your church does have individual teachers make those purchases, then be sure you have a system for quick reimbursement of the money spent.

While many churches have a library which is used by children, youth, and adults, some churches choose to keep books which may be borrowed available in each classroom. Whatever procedure you use, be certain that teachers understand how they and their class members can check out those books. An individual with an appreciation for books needs to be in charge of these resources, ordering new ones as appropriate and "retiring" those which are out of date.

Some churches are in the process of developing media libraries of cassette tapes, CDs, posters, and videotapes. Those materials need to be kept in an orderly arrangement so it is easy for teachers to find resources they can use. Unless your church has tape or CD players and VCR players for each classroom, there is a need to have a check-out system for those pieces of equipment. Your church may well choose not to have a media library or resource center, but you at least want to have ready access to catalogs of media resources which can be borrowed or rented from denominational agencies, local libraries, and various media companies.

10.When teachers want to quit, let them quit. Make it clear that teaching assignments are only for a year at a time. If you take this approach, it is important to give everyone a card in the spring (if your new educational year starts in the fall) to see how many will continue. It is generally best to hand deliver those cards during the week or to mail them to the homes of teachers. If you distribute the cards on Sunday morning (or at the meeting time of a Sunday evening or midweek group), the success or failure of that particular day will largely determine the response. Persons who have been greatly frustrated with a class will be ready to resign as soon as they see the card. It's better for them to receive the card later in the week when they can look at their teaching experiences on balance rather than from a particular day's perspective.

When persons agree to teach in the coming year, respond with a letter, phone call, or visit letting them know that their continued service is appreciated. When persons resign, contact them by a phone call or a visit to acknowledge acceptance of the resignation. At the time of that phone call or visit, ask them to share with you the reason or reasons for resigning. Don't use this as an opportunity to "talk them out" of the decision, but rather as a means to better understand what has happened. If the resignation is because of changes in personal or family life or because of the need for a change of pace, there is nothing further you need to do. If the resignation is because of discipline problems in the class, problems with curriculum materials, or other difficulties, then that information needs to be used by the education commission to prevent the same problems from happening again.

Job Descriptions Help Everyone with Outreach

Concept: If no one is responsible for it, no one will do it. If everyone if responsible for it, no one will do it. Job descriptions are a necessary part of efforts to reach out through Christian education.

Job descriptions are boring to many people, and it's also true that they aren't frequently read, even in many businesses. Not having job descriptions, however, means that too many needs fall through the cracks of the church's organizational structure. If a particular task is assigned to everyone or to no one, it is safe to assume that no one will do it. The church's educational ministry in general, and efforts at outreach in particular, are too important to be left to chance.

Every church needs a board, committee, or commission which has overall responsibility for educational programming in the church. That group should have the final word in decisions about curriculum and policy. They should also be the group which sets goals for growth and encourages others to be involved in the process.

The job descriptions shared in this section have been actively used and tested in several local churches, each of which made a few modifications. You'll need to adapt them for your particular local church's organizational structure, but they may give you some helpful starting places. Note that the job descriptions for teachers specify not only what teachers are asked to do, but also what the church (through the Board of Education, the counseling teachers, and the superintendent) will do to support the teachers.

Once you develop the habit of sharing job descriptions or a handbook which contains job descriptions with teachers, board of education members, and others, you'll find that it makes a positive difference in the willingness of people to accept positions of responsibility.

The Board of Education
And Its Members

1.   are responsible for the total educational program of the church including the Sunday school and the youth groups.

2.   make decisions on curriculum materials. It is important that consistency be maintained in curriculum at the children's level. Youth and adult classes should normally be given more freedom in selecting their own materials and topics.

3.   should provide annual orientation for church school teachers and youth group advisors.

4.   offer winter and spring workshops for teachers and advisors.

5.   promote involvement in denominational and ecumenical workshops, mini-labs, lab schools, and retreats which would be of value to teachers and advisors.

6.   develop and update a booklet or manual for the church school which includes:

- job descriptions for all educational positions.

- the name, address, phone number, and position for each educational worker.

- dates and times of any projected workshops, meetings, or special emphases including fall orientation, Rally Day, Christian Education Sunday, winter and spring workshops, and Board of Education meeting dates.

- information about substitute teachers.

• information about purchasing materials, ordering curriculum, and obtaining videotapes and other media resources.

7. see that short term study opportunities are offered during the year.

8. recruit teachers, advisors, and other educational workers on an annual basis.

9. plan an annual recognition of all teachers and education workers.

10. develop a plan of follow-up on persons who become inactive in classes and groups.

11. plan *at least* an annual emphasis on attendance with the aim of involving new persons in the Sunday school and in youth groups. This could take the form of a Rally Day with phone calls and personal visits to promote attendance. This emphasis should have Church Board approval and should include help from the Evangelism Committee.

12. see that weekly attendance records are maintained and that the figures are reported to the church office for use in monitoring attendance trends and for the annual report to the denominational offices.

13. set annual goals for growth in the educational program and work cooperatively with all teachers and with the Evangelism Committee to see that those goals are met.

14. see that new youth and adult classes and groups are offered as needed.

15. purchase and make available needed videotapes, books, craft materials, and other resources.

16. encourage the creative use of media in classes.

17. ensure a system of support for and communication with all teachers, advisors, and other educational workers.

18. provide at least an annual evaluation of needed physical improvements and share those recommendations with the Trustees and Church Board.

19. submit an annual budget to the Church Board.

20. coordinate activities with other groups in the church, especially the Christmas and Easter observances.

The Superintendent of Study

1. is a member of the Board of Education.

2. coordinates the work of the counseling teachers and assists them wherever possible.

3. provides Sunday morning supervision of church school activities or ensures that this supervision is provided by the counseling teachers.

4. ensures that attendance records are picked up from each class each week and that those records are given to the church office.

5. helps the Board of Education recruit teachers and leaders and involves the counseling teachers in that process.

6. sees that the minister and the Board of Education are kept informed of needs, problems, *and successes* in the Sunday school.

Counseling Teachers

1. are members of the Board of Education.

2. communicate policies, programs, and concerns of the Board of Education to teachers.

3.   ensure that the Board of Education is aware of the problems and needs of teachers.

4.   offer help to teachers in dealing with discipline problems, planning problems, obtaining media and other resources, and using curriculum materials.

5.   help teachers follow up on persons who become inactive.

6.   keep the minister aware of new children, youth, or young adults who attend Sunday school.

7.   share with the teachers information from the minister about prospective members who should be contacted about class or group opportunities. Follow up to be sure the contacts have been made and give assistance in those contacts if needed.

8.   find substitutes when teachers must be absent. Developing a list of persons willing to substitute may be the best approach.

9.   contact the teachers of all assigned classes each spring to determine which ones will continue in the fall. Then accept the primary responsibility for recruiting new teachers for the classes assigned.

10. visit informally with teachers to give support, share appreciation, find out about new needs, etc.

11. recruit teachers for involvement in workshops and special emphases.

12. ensure that curriculum orders are placed with the Resource Secretary.

Possible assignments to counseling teachers:
- Nursery & Kindergarten
- Lower Elementary
- Upper Elementary
- Youth
- Adult

The Resource Secretary

1. maintains in good condition the Church Library, which is by the sanctuary, and the Resource Library, which is in the educational wing.

2. orders appropriate materials for the Church Library and the Resource Library, keeping within the budget limits of the Board of Education and seeking suggestions from the church staff, the superintendent of study, the counseling teachers, and the classroom teachers.

3. requests curriculum orders from the counseling teachers and classroom teachers comfortably before the ordering deadline each quarter, places those orders, and sees that the materials are properly distributed.

4. helps the counseling teachers and classroom teachers obtain needed media resources.

5. helps with the fall orientation of teachers by providing information on curriculum ordering and on media resources.

6. attends the state Christian Education Media Fair each year and brings back a list of new media resources to share with the counseling teachers and classroom teachers.

Sunday School Teachers

are asked to:

1. attend the fall orientation meeting.

2. be present each Sunday or notify the counseling teacher as far in advance as possible.

3. be well prepared each Sunday using the curriculum resources approved by the Board of Education.

4. share problems, needs, and ideas with the counseling teacher assigned.

5.   maintain regular attendance records on each student, and provide a total count each Sunday (along with a report of absences) to the Superintendent of Study or the person designated by the Superintendent.

6.   write or (preferably) phone students who miss two consecutive weeks; phone those who miss three consecutive weeks; and visit those who miss four consecutive weeks.   The counseling teacher will help you if needed.

7.   notify the counseling teacher of any students who miss more than four consecutive weeks.

8.   share invitations to class with prospective members when notified of that need by the counseling teacher, and encourage class members to do the same.

9.   attend the winter and spring workshops.

10. attend other announced training events or enrichment opportunities when possible.

11. attend morning worship and encourage class members to do the same.

Your church will support you by:

1.   providing a substitute when you need to be gone.

2.   providing the orientation each fall as well as the winter and spring workshops.

3.   providing adequate craft, curriculum, and media resources and being responsive to your requests for new materials.

4.   having a counseling teacher and the superintendent of study available for guidance, help, and encouragement.

5.   asking you well in advance whether you wish to teach again next year.

6.   giving you a subscription to a Christian education newsletter.

Employed Staff And Christian Education

```
CONCEPT: Employed staff members can play
an important role in Christian education if
everyone involved understands that role.
```

Most local churches are relatively small and are served by only one minister or priest. Some local churches are so small that they must share pastoral leadership with one or two other congregations. Yet there are many churches large enough to have a part-time or full-time professional staff member who works in the area of Christian education. Consider the options:

- A minister or priest who serves as an associate and who specializes in Christian education or accepts that as a major responsibility.

- A Christian Education Director, who may have received almost as much seminary education as a local church pastor, or who may come to the church from a background of work in secular education.

- A part-time staff member who has some skills in Christian education.

- A parish visitor who will devote a certain percentage of time to calls on behalf of the educational program.

While the ideal would be a minister, priest, or seminary trained director, many persons who have had less theological training may still do an excellent job. In a person to work with Christian education, you want someone who:

- Accepts and is willing to support the main position of your denomination on theological matters.

- Knows how to plan and organize an effective educational program working cooperatively with the committee or commission responsible for education, with teachers, and with others concerned about that program.

- Knows how to use the telephone to coordinate plans and messages.

- Is willing to make personal visits to potential members and to the homes of inactive members.

- Genuinely likes people and has the ability to communicate that warmth.

- Understands how to and can help others use curriculum materials and media resources.

- Is personally a good teacher and can demonstrate a variety of teaching styles.

- Has a good understanding of the needs of various age levels and of the dynamics of modern family life.

The presence of a staff member in Christian education will only help your program grow *if volunteers can be persuaded not to expect the staff member to do everything.* The staff member's major energies should be going to the preparation of new programs, teacher training, and the direct teaching of some classes or studies. The staff member should be involved in visiting prospective members and persons who have become inactive, but those contacts cannot take the place of visits made by the regular teachers of classes and groups. It's unfair to expect that individual to make a multitude of phone calls for every teacher in the church school. Likewise, don't expect this person to maintain all the educational records without secretarial or volunteer help. Many churches have added an educational staff person only to have relatively little growth in the program because that staff person had to spend much of his or her time doing what volunteers did before.

Local churches have traditionally done an inadequate job providing financial support to Christian education directors, music directors, youth workers, and business administrators. The general attitude seems to be to hire the person for as little as possible, work the person as hard as possible, and retire the person with as little pension as possible. Those kinds of routine policies by a local church are unquestionably wrong and also discourage talented people from going into Christian education. A church which is looking for a professional in Christian education, whether part-time or full-time, should be searching for the best-qualified individual and should be prepared to pay a fair salary.

Even without a staff member who specializes in Christian education, the pastor of the church constitutes an extremely valuable resource to the educational program. Whenever possible, the minister or another staff person assigned to Christian education should:

• Meet with the education committee or commission to provide counsel and direction in developing the educational ministry of the church.

• Be available to counsel individually with teachers and youth advisors as needed. Seminary training offers background information and valuable perspective on many issues of importance to the church and its members. There will be some biblical and theological questions which the minister is best qualified to address.

• Teach long- and short-term classes. The minister or other seminary-trained staff persons have a great deal to offer through teaching because of the biblical and theological background provided in a good seminary education. In most growing churches, ministers and other staff members take seriously their own teaching responsibility.

• Call in the homes of persons who have dropped out of regular activity. The initial attempts at reactivating these persons should come from the teachers and the education commission or committee, but the minister needs to follow up when there has been no response to home visits by lay people.

•   Link the education commission or committee, teachers, and youth advisors to resource persons and opportunities in the denomination and to ecumenical opportunities in the area.

•   Help the education commission or committee organize and carry out local church orientations and workshops for teachers and youth advisors.

•   Take special interest in the youth program of the church. There is a clear positive relationship between the involvement of the minister and the success of the youth program. At the same time, it is important that the minister not be the advisor for every youth group, or those programs may not survive the departure of the minister.

Part Three:

Reaching Out
By Building Attendance

Most of the suggestions in Part Two on Reaching
Out Through Leadership should result in increased
attendance. In Part Three, we'll look more specifi-
cally at ways to increase attendance at Christian
education programs and events. Increased attendance almost always results in increased membership and financial support and will also strengthen
the church's ability to reach out on issues of peace
and justice.

I told him: "My children and I were in Sunday school class for two years. Then we went through a difficult time, and I couldn't handle the transportation. I kept hoping someone from the church would reach out to us, but no one did. I know I could have taken the initiative to ask for help, but I thought surely someone would think of us and ask why we weren't coming."

A Single Mother

Maintain Those Lists!

CONCEPT: You can't reach out to people if you don't know who they are or where they are!

Many churches neglect membership and attendance records, but they do so at great cost. Each Christian education class or group needs an up to date class roster which includes the name, address, phone, emergency information (in the event of illness when parents are gone), and attendance record of each class or group participant.

When it is clear that someone is no longer active, then proceed in this way:

- See that a pastoral call and a volunteer call are made on that person.

- If there is no positive result, place the name in an inactive file. Don't drop the name unless you learn that the person is attending another church.

- Periodically (once or twice a year), go through the inactive file and make another effort at contacting those persons.

- Be sure that any information gained from contacts with inactive persons is shared with the pastor.

The next section talks in greater detail about the importance of prompt follow-up when there has been a break in the attendance pattern of any person.

Keep Them Coming

CONCEPT: No single action helps educational programs grow as much as prompt follow-up on absences.

Regardless of the quality of your educational programs, some people will become inactive. This includes new class members who have only attended a few times and persons who have grown up in the church. Don't wait too long before responding to any change in a person's attendance or activity pattern.

Several studies have been conducted on the relationship between the first few absences and the move to chronic inactivity. Whether one is dealing with Protestant or Catholic congregations, children or adults, large congregation or small congregation, it remains clear that *there is a direct relationship between the promptness of response to the initial break in attendance pattern and the probability that the person will return to active involvement*.

If you wait as long as six months to respond to the absence of a student, the probability of that person's returning to regular attendance is between 24% and 32%. If you follow up on the break in attendance pattern within six weeks, the probability of return rises to 90%. These figures exclude those instances when a person is absent because of travel plans or illness.

The kind of response chosen is also important. In general, phone calls are the most successful initial approach. Letters are usually not successful and can be interpreted as critical, and a personal visit may be an overreaction if the break in attendance has been relatively brief. A phone call gives the opportunity to share that the person has been missed and to inquire whether or not there is any problem. If the phone call does not bring a return to attendance within a couple of weeks, then a personal visit is in order.

Letters and postcards do work better with elementary children than with youth or adults. A phone call would still be the preferred response; but if leader time is limited, a personally written note or card is a satisfactory first step with elementary children. The message of the note or card should not convey any blame but simply the sentiment of the child having been missed. If the card or letter does not bring a return to attendance within a week, then make a phone call.

The follow-up on the absence of preschoolers should be made with the parents and by phone. Handle the situation as you would if the adult had been absent from an adult class.

Don't Leave It to Chance

Don't leave follow-up on absences to chance. Keep a record of attendance. If the same person is absent two or three consecutive weeks and there is no apparent reason, a member of the group or the teacher should call. Don't be critical of the absence, but do make it clear that the person was genuinely missed. Simply affirm your interest and express the hope that he or she will be present for the next class or meeting. If a second or third contact becomes necessary, then you need to discover the reason for the change in activity, probably through a personal visit.

Another word is appropriate concerning cards or notes to elementary children. You will find a wide range available from many denominational curriculum outlets and through other supply houses. Choose the ones which are humorous or express concern. Don't choose cards which shame, blame, or poke fun at the person who has been absent. There is a difference between humor and ridicule! It's hard to believe that people actually buy some of the obnoxious cards that are stocked. Send the kind of card you would like to receive! And remember, again, that a phone call is still the preferred initial contact.

If your approaches to a child or young person are not successful, then you may wish to contact the parents. You should not contact the parents with the aim of having them punish the child or make the young person come; the most that will gain you is an angry class member. A better approach is to ask the parents if they know why their son or daughter no longer attends and if a they have any suggestions for you. This involves them in talking about the situation, and they may be able to help with positive encouragement from their end.

The responsibility for follow-up on absences needs to be assigned. The teacher or teachers of the class should be responsible for keeping a record of attendance, unless that task has been assigned to a secretary in an adult class. The responsibility for follow-up on absences may be assigned to:

- a counseling teacher or a superintendent for that age level. The teacher is responsible for contacting that person.

- a task force or committee of the church which is concerned with education or evangelism. Again, the teacher must be responsible for sharing news of the absence.

- a member of the class. Youth and adult groups may wish to rotate this responsibility. In some instances, it may be more natural for a person living in the same neighborhood to make the contact.

- the teacher of the class. This is not a difficult task, since most follow-ups can be accomplished with a phone call. The matter is made easier if a team of teachers works with each class or group.

With very few exceptions, it is best for a member of the class or a teacher of the class to make the contact. Having other persons make the contact is less personal and may appear like a legalistic approach. A member of the class or a teacher of the class can genuinely make the contact as an expression of interest and friendship.

Classes and groups within the church should provide caring, supportive environments. One way of reinforcing that kind of environment is to emphasize group concern and responsibility for a person who is no longer coming.

Think about the Results

Regular follow-up on absences can have significant impact. Most Sunday schools, youth groups, CCD classes, and other educational groups have peak attendance in the fall and again in Lent. Those are also the times of the year when persons who do not belong to the church are most likely to start coming. The fall and Lenten figures are generally about the same in size, but they often represent a shift in class members. Ten to 15 percent of those who attend in the fall will break the attendance pattern and will not return to regular attendance for several years (if at all).

That 10%-15% is compensated for during Lent by new persons who begin attending (either potential members or previously inactive members). The simple act of following up on non-attenders can keep the church from losing the 10%-15% in the fall. Since the new 10%-15% will still begin coming in the Lenten season, the net result can be a significant gain in average attendance for the church's educational program. We often miss the significance of this because 10%-15% of a given class may only be one, two, or three people. The accumulative result of this, however, is impressive. In a large church, good follow-up on breaks in attendance can result in 10% church school growth; over five years of time that can result in a 50% increase. (Note that these figures exclude those persons who simply move out of the community.)

Consider how attendance ran in one small youth group:

Fall	Winter	Lent	Summer	Fall
Bob	Bob	Bob	Bob	Bob
Dick				
Mike	Mike	Mike	Mike	Mike
Alice	Alice	Alice	Alice	Alice
Betty	Betty	Betty	Betty	Betty
Kathy		Kathy		Kathy
Sarah				
		Alan		
		Kris		

None of the young people were seniors, so graduation did not explain the failure of four young people who had been active

87

sometime during the year to be active the following fall. None of the young people moved. That local church increased its average youth group attendance by sixty percent the following year by instituting a regular follow-up program.

A variety of studies consistently show that the percentage of people on the member or constituency rolls of the church who are present in Sunday school on a typical Sunday declines significantly with age. A LifeQuest study shows the following percentages of each indicated age level present on a typical Sunday morning:

Kindergarten through Second Grade	**64%**
Third Grade through Sixth Grade	**55%**
Seventh Grade through Eighth Grade	**51%**
Ninth Grade through Twelfth Grade	**43%**
18-22 Years of Age	**21%**
Twenty-three Years of Age and Older	**29%**

Obviously at the younger age levels, in most denominational traditions, we are talking about constituents rather than members. Depending on the denominational policy and on the local church practice, most people are confirmed as members sometime between the sixth grade and twelfth grade. For the purposes of this study, constituents as well as members were included at each age level, since constituents generally represent prospective members. The overall rate of decline is huge, even given the fact that some adults return to activity at a later time. It should also be noted that today's young adults are less likely to return to activity with the event of marriage or the birth of a first child than in some previous generations.

Repeated studies by many denominations have confirmed that a large number of people quit coming to church classes and groups because they do not have a strong feeling of acceptance; because they have been offended in some way (often without the knowledge of those who did the offending); or because they do not feel that their ideas are appreciated. Follow-up on non-attenders is a way of saying to them that they are accepted and that their involvement is important. It is also a way of opening up conversation if someone is hurt or offended.

A single parent expressed what she said to her minister about the hurt and frustration she felt when her church did not respond to the break in attendance of her children and of herself:

> I told him: "My children and I were in Sunday school
> class for two years. Then we went through a difficult
> time, and I couldn't handle the transportation. I
> kept hoping someone from the church would reach
> out to us, but no one did. I know I could have
> taken the initiative to ask for help, but I thought
> surely someone would think of us and ask why
> we weren't coming."

Unfortunately the minister received that information four years
after the difficult time she had experienced, and she no longer
had interest in returning to that local church. Absence can be a
cry for help, which will go unheard if there is no procedure for
follow-up.

That follow-up initially needs to come from class members,
teachers, and other volunteers rather than from the professional
staff of the church. The minister or other professional staff
members should generally not be asked to call on the inactive
person unless contacts from the class reveal a problem which
should have professional attention. Most professional
employees of local churches are badly overworked and cannot
follow up on every break in attendance which occurs. A staff
member should be involved when there are obvious family
problems; when there is anger toward the church that is not
being resolved; when a member of the household is seriously ill;
or when someone is threatening to leave the church.

More Thoughts on Keeping Them Coming

Following up on absences is extremely important, but it's
even better if people can be helped to have such a strong feeling
of belonging to a class or group that they don't want to miss any
sessions or meetings. The following strategies have been effective
in many classes and groups:

- Be sure that visitors and new class members are
  introduced to everyone and genuinely helped to
  feel accepted by the group.

- Take steps to ensure that visitors to the class
  are contacted during the week - ideally not only

by a teacher or leader but also by a member of
the class.

- Have refreshments available at the start of
  class, since this provides an excellent opportunity
  for informal socializing. This is especially true
  for adult classes and has also been practiced
  with success at the youth and children's
  levels. [Donuts and cookies work well with all
  age levels. Coffee and tea are generally best
  with adults, and fruit juices or drinks work with
  children and youth.]

- Have some social events for class members which
  provide opportunity for stronger bonds to be
  developed.

- Provide opportunities for class or group members
  to share in meaningful service projects. This can
  be important outreach on behalf of Christ and
  the church, and working together generally
  strengthens the bonds of the group.

Getting the Word Out

> **CONCEPT:** Use every means possible to let others know what your church is doing in Christian education.

Studies across denominational lines continue to confirm that the majority of people try out a given local church because a friend, co-worker, neighbor, or acquaintance invited them to do so. That doesn't mean other strategies can't be effective, but we do well to remember that reality as we plan strategies to reach new members for the Christian education program and for the church. The most effective strategies will normally be those which encourage people who are already active in the church to share invitations with others.

Many people, of course, are not overly confident about sharing their faith with others or about inviting others to attend church. We can make that process easier for people by strategies such as:

• Using class or group time to have members role play or rehearse the process of inviting someone to Sunday school, a small group, or worship.

• Providing devotional booklets, descriptive brochures, or other materials which members can hand to those who might be interested in the church. Having something specific to share can make it easier to begin a conversation.

• Giving people opportunity to share in tasks like taking freshly baked cookies or bread to people who have visited the church or who are prospective

members. This is an enjoyable task and makes
it easier to start conversations.

• Having people share in neighborhood canvasses or
surveys. It's easier to approach people one doesn't
know well as part of an overall church program
than on one's own.

• Letting people work in pairs where possible, so
that mutual support can be offered.

• Providing books like *Plain Talk About Church Growth*
and *Overcoming Barriers To Church Growth* which
can help people better understand how to approach
others.

With the preceding ideas as background, consider the
programs, ideas, and strategies which follow as possibilities for
your church.

• Develop a leaflet or brochure which members can
give to their friends and which can also be given
to those who visit your church. A theme such as
"We Care About Children" can be excellent in
approaching young families. Even if a brochure
already exists describing your church as a whole,
consider the possibility of a separate brochure
which highlights work with children. Depending
on the size of your church, separate brochures
may also be helpful on youth and young adult
opportunities in your church.

• Use Invite-a-Friend Sundays or Rally Days as
special occasions when everyone in the church
is encouraged to invite friends, neighbors,
co-workers, and family to worship services and
Sunday school. Develop special fliers and postcards which members can share with those being
invited. Don't leave children's classes out of
the process. Children are often the most
enthusiastic about inviting others to join them
at church.

• Organize a visitation program to every household

in the neighborhood (or neighborhoods) being served by your church. Have volunteers introduce themselves, share their relationship with your church, and ask about the church connection of those on whom they are calling. If those persons have no church home, then visit about the opportunities at your church and leave a brochure and other information. Some churches like to take along a short devotional booklet and give it to all households, regardless of church affiliation.

• Bus ministries are still effective in some parts of the country, but there is nothing guaranteed about a bus ministry except that it will cost you a lot of money! The most effective bus ministries are those in which the bus drivers go around neighborhoods on Saturday and ask children, young people, and adults if they would like a ride the next day. If these ministries are done with integrity, those persons who indicate they are involved in another church should be left alone.

• Posters and banners at strategic locations around your community can be a good way to focus attention on specific programs of your church.

• Consider radio and television spot announcements if local station policies and your church's financial resources make that realistic. Local cable TV station announcements are often not effective, so it may be better to pay the price of a short spot on a local network affiliate. Focusing your announcement on the needs of children or youth can be a valuable way to set your church apart from others. Some denominations provide tapes to which your own church's identification can be added.

• Local cable TV station announcements may not be helpful, but cable TV programs done by your church may bring results. The announcement only lasts between fifteen seconds and three minutes. A program may be thirty minutes or longer. You need to deal with issues which are of fairly broad interest in order to gain the

cooperation of the cable company. Consider
programs on topics like youth violence, drugs,
local hunger concerns, and developing the
spiritual life.

• Newspaper advertising can help in some situations.
Church advertisements on the sports page or in
the features section generally do much better than
in the religious section.

• Yellow page advertising is extremely important.
This is the main place most new residents will
look if they are actively searching for a church
home. How large an advertisement you
purchase depends on your church budget,
but the following features and information
are helpful when possible:

- Have a box placed around the advertisement,
which increases readership.

- Include the times of your worship service or services
and of Sunday school or other continuing Christian
education activities. If you have a different summer
schedule, either include that schedule or indicate
that the church office should be called for the
summer schedule. A large number of persons
looking for a church home will be doing so in the
summer months at the conclusion of the moving
process.

- Indicate that child care is provided (if it is!).

- If your church has ramps for wheelchairs, also
indicate that in your advertisement.

- Clearly indicate where people may phone for more
information, and then be certain the information
really will be available if they call for it.

Surveys can be a good way to gain valuable information
about the people you seek to serve while giving active members a
comfortable opportunity to interact with persons who are not
members of your church. The following survey was developed for

use by teenagers in reaching out to other youth in the community. The survey results provide useful information on the kinds of programming which might be helpful, and the process of asking others the questions can generate meaningful discussions. A slightly different version of this survey appears in the book *Peer Evangelism* by Steve Clapp and Sam Detwiler. You have permission to reproduce these questions for use in your local church.

Those conducting the survey should be instructed to explain the process in words similar to these: "My church is trying to better understand the opinions, the values, and the needs of teenagers in our community. It would help if you could answer a few questions for us." While people could simply be handed a printed copy of the survey to complete, it will generate more discussion and be more helpful if the church member asks the questions of the other person. While twenty-five questions may appear to be a lot, the actual time to complete the survey is relatively brief unless it causes interesting discussion.

What Do You Think?

Name:

Phone:

These first questions ask about your likes and dislikes, your preferences.

1. Who is your favorite film star?

2. Who is your favorite musician or musical group?

3. What is the best motion picture you've seen this year?

4. What is your favorite television program?

5. What is your favorite form of recreation?

These questions seek your opinion about some issues and problems in our community.

What percentage of students in your school do you think:

6.   ... have used illegal drugs?

7.   ... have used tobacco products?

8.   ... drink alcoholic beverages?

9.   ... have cheated on a test?

10. ... have already had sexual intercourse?

11. ... have shoplifted?

12. ... have been the victim of a crime?

13. ... have trouble handling anger and hostility?

14. ... have themselves hurt another person?

15. ... don't have enough money to dress well and feel comfortable around other teens?

16. What would you say are the two major areas in which teenagers in our community need help?

Naturally our church is concerned about the extent to which people find religious faith helpful in dealing with life. The next group of questions deals with these concerns.

17. Do you belong to a church or other religious organization? If so, which one?

18. How often do you attend religious activities?
    a. twice a week   b. weekly
    c. 2-3 times a month   d. monthly
    e. only on special occasions   f. never

19. Do you think prayer can help solve problems?

20. Do you think prayer can help you grow closer to God?

21. How much do you know about the Bible?
    a. a whole lot   b. a lot   c. some   d. not very much

22. Would you like to know more about the Bible?

23. Would you like to feel closer to God?

24. Would you ever be interested in attending a spiritual life retreat?

25. Would you ever be interested in joining a Bible study group?

Variations on the survey can be used with upper elementary youth and with young adults. You may wish to substitute issues or concerns which are of special importance in your community at the present time.

As you can see, compiling the survey results will produce an interesting view of teenagers in the community. The results, with the names of survey participants of course not revealed, could be used for newspaper articles or even radio and television programming, depending on the openness of the media in your community. The responses from those persons who are not active in a local church should give you many ideas for creative programming to reach out to them.

Attendance and Participation Awards

CONCEPT: Symbolic gifts for all group members can strengthen commitment and loyalty. Awards for attendance and other accomplishments can be valuable but do have a downside.

In earlier decades, attendance awards were frequently presented to Sunday school students in Protestant churches. The awards were generally in the form of a lapel pin with bars which could be hung from the bottom of the pin with each additional year of perfect attendance. Many churches continue to give such awards, but the practice is not as widespread as previously.

Part of the reason for attendance awards no longer being presented in many churches is the simple reality that increased weekend mobility means that fewer people qualify for the awards! There are, however, some downsides to attendance awards and to some other forms of recognition which should be identified before considering the positive uses of these strategies:

- Those receiving awards can develop a "I'm better than you" spirit which drives off less-committed and newer students.

- With some children, the attainment of the award becomes the purpose for attending educational

activities. This can cause the matter of growing
in the Christian faith to move into secondary
importance.

- Family travel plans and illness can disqualify
students who may feel cheated because they
have little control over plans made by their
parents and no control over illness.

Attendance award programs should be developed with clearly
stated but flexible expectations. Provision should be made for
days missed because of illness, and there may be merit in
allowing "make up" credits through Vacation Bible School,
special Lenten studies, or other program participation to help
class members who miss because of travel. The atmosphere
created by the teachers should be one which encourages perfect
attendance, but which does not make that the exclusive goal of
the Christian education process! Visitors and new class
members should be helped to feel part of the group and not to
feel "second class" because they do not yet have awards; the
award can become a goal to encourage attendance by new
members. With those provisions in place, attendance awards
can be a valuable part of your program.
Most Christian education programs should also give careful
consideration to other kinds of recognition and symbolic gifts
which reinforce membership, participation, and excellence.
Consider the following possibilities:

- T-shirts for all the members of a Sunday school
class at the children's and youth levels. These can
be distinctive for each age level - perhaps sweat
shirts for teenagers. Involve class members in the
design process. These reinforce participation for
those in the class and also reinforce group
identification when presented to new group
members.

- Have distinctive name tags or membership pins
which are given to members of a youth or adult
class (or small group or choir).

- Some churches develop a distinctive pin which
is given to all church members. These are
presented to new members on completion of

the membership class and preparation process.

- Give promotional certificates to children at
  the time they progress from one grade level
  to the next. If these are attractively prepared,
  many children and parents will keep them
  for years.

- Many churches have a tradition of presenting
  a Bible to children when they reach a certain
  grade level. Build on that helpful tradition
  by presenting a Bible handbook or a prayer
  resource at another age level.

Awards and prizes can also be shared for bringing new people into classes and groups. Rather than awarding these on an individual basis, consider recognition for the whole class when a particular goal in membership growth or average attendance has been accomplished. Recognition might be through the awarding of pens or mugs for each group member or through a pizza party or other special event for the group.

In the award and recognition process, don't overlook those who teach and provide other kinds of leadership. Consider, for example:

- Having a special commissioning service at the
  start of the program year which recognizes all
  teachers and at which they are presented with
  a pin or book.

- Sharing a gift of appreciation such as a pen,
  mug, bookmark, or carefully chosen book with
  each teacher at the conclusion of the program
  year.

- Creating a "Teacher of the Year" award for those
  who have demonstrated excellence in teaching.
  Such traditions can be good motivators, but
  it's also important to use the award presentation
  as an opportunity to extend appreciation to
  ALL teachers rather than letting it become a
  time when some feel overlooked. The person
  receiving the award needs to be one whom almost
  everyone will recognize as deserving because of

years of service or especially outstanding achieve-
ment. If someone does not stand out that
clearly, it's better not to present the award.
In general, we prefer other kinds of recognition;
but this strategy is used successfully in many
churches.

• Having a special brunch or reception for teachers
  at the start of the program year, at Christmas,
  at Easter, or at the end of the program year.
  It doesn't hurt to have this kind of event more
  than once during the year!

• Having certificates presented to teachers who
  complete laboratory school or other training
  programs.

• Being sure to honor those who "retire" from
  teaching after many years of involvement.
  Such occasions provide opportunities to
  celebrate the accomplishments of all teachers.

Also remember, as was shared in the chapter on "Teacher
Training, Support, and Reinforcement" that the best possible
motivators to teachers are genuinely felt, informal words of
encouragement. The same is true for members of classes and
groups. Class name tags, pins, T-shirts, sweatshirts, hats, and
other symbolic gifts can be valuable; but nothing replaces or is
even equal to the knowledge that one's participation is valued by
the teacher and by other group members.

Also keep in mind that times of sickness or personal
problems often test the extent to which group members really
care about one another. Following up on an absence, as
discussed in other chapters, is really a way of saying that the
individual is important to the group. When there are problems
in a person's life, the group may be moved to respond; and those
responses warrant encouragement. I think in particular of:

• A church member who had a tragic accident and
  was hospitalized for several months. Members of
  a Sunday school class helped the family with
  child care and food and made regular visits to the
  person in the hospital. Although most were not
  aware of it, that family had been considering

leaving the church. Their importance to the Christian community was reinforced, and their own bond to that community was strengthened. They did not leave the church and in fact became heavily involved in inviting others to the church.

•   An elderly couple had an adult child who was seriously ill in a distant city. They wanted to travel there to be with the child and to help with the care of grandchildren, but they could not afford to make the trip. It was mentioned as a prayer concern at the start of a Sunday school class, and group members took a spontaneous offering which paid for the couple's travel.

•   A child lost a leg when hit by an automobile. Sunday school class members were concerned, but also felt uncomfortable with the situation. The teachers of the children helped them express their anxieties and think about how their friend must feel. They visited in the hospital as a group and then set up a schedule to spend time with their friend after dismissal from the hospital. Their reaching out proved of great value to the injured friend, to that friend's parents, and to everyone in the group.

That kind of reaching out flows from the church, the body of Christ, at its best. No pin, T-shirt, certificate, or mug can convey what those actions did.

Vacation Bible School

CONCEPT: Although some things have changed over the years, Vacation Bible School remains one of the best outreach strategies for many local churches.

For many years, Vacation Bible School or Vacation Church School was an accepted, regular part of the local church's program. In some communities, VBS was a multi-denominational project with the involvement of two or more different congregations. We are now in a period of time in which many churches do not offer VBS and in which others are having difficulty continuing the tradition. This reality seems especially unfortunate since 1994 is the 100th anniversary of Vacation Bible School! There are several reasons for the current difficulties with VBS:

* With increasing numbers of households being single parent or having both husband and wife employed, the available pool of volunteers for a major enterprise like VBS is not as large as in the past.

* Some churches have experienced such diminished numbers of children in the Sunday school that there do not seem to be enough available to come to justify the energy of VBS.

* The strongest VBS programs of the past tended to be in churches to which large numbers of

children would walk from their homes. The
neighborhood ties of many churches are no
longer so strong, and transportation problems
for children who attend are a more significant
issue. Concerns about safety have also made
parents in the neighborhood more reluctant
to let their children walk unsupervised to the
church.

Because of those realities, VBS will not work in every
situation. The outreach possibilities of a good VBS program,
however, are significant:

• Most unchurched households are more likely
to permit a child to attend VBS for one or two
weeks than to make a regular commitment to
getting the child to Sunday school.

• Some churches have experimented with VBS
in the evening and have found unchurched
adults open to attending seminars or workshops
conducted in conjunction with VBS. This
can provide an excellent port of entry to the
church for the whole family.

• Households with single parents or with both
parents employed sometimes find attractive
a VBS program which relieves them of the
child care arrangement responsibility for
part of the summer.

With good follow-up efforts, many unchurched families can
be persuaded to make the transition from VBS to regular Sunday
school and worship attendance. The quality of what happens
during VBS and the intentionality of follow-up by the church
determine whether or not that transition occurs.

Here are some possibilities to consider in organizing a
Vacation Bible School for your church:

• Even if your church membership is not strongly
based in the neighborhood around the church,
consider reaching out to that neighborhood with
VBS. Have volunteers distribute fliers door-to-door
and visit informally with people where appropriate.

- Encourage children to bring their friends to VBS. Provide an attractive flier that they can share.

- Consider the possibility of an evening VBS, which makes possible a larger pool of volunteers and also permits you to experiment more readily with seminars and workshops for adults.

- Be sure to maintain careful records for VBS. You want to have names, addresses, and phone numbers for new children, youth, and adults who attend. Then follow-up visits can be made to encourage those persons to try the regular Sunday school and worship opportunities at your church.

- Depending on your situation, day camp may be an alternative to VBS. Consider offering the camp at a local park, and have a variety of activities which last half-a-day or all day. In some communities, day camp opportunities are more popular than traditional VBS.

- Most churches find it difficult to interest senior high youth in attending VBS, and those senior high who are employed may not be able to attend during the day. Consider using available senior highs as assistants or helpers with children's classes. Most senior highs don't have the life experience or teaching experience needed to be lead teachers, but they can give good service as assistants and also learn a lot in the process.

- Include class or total VBS photographs as part of the program. Also consider giving T-shirts or some other item to all who participate. Those are tangible reminders of the good experiences at VBS and help people think about the church in the year ahead.

Teaching People To Share Their Faith

CONCEPT: Many church members and active constituents fail to share their faith with others because they don't feel comfortable with the process.

Some approaches to evangelism are just plain uncomfortable for many church members, especially within mainline Protestant, Anabaptist, and Catholic congregations. Many people associate evangelism with:

- Asking others: "Are you saved?"

- Telling people the "four spiritual laws" or some other variation of a simple process for finding God (which has to be memorized in order to be told correctly).

- Wearing a fake smile plastered to the face.

When that is the image of evangelism and faith-sharing which people hold, they may understandably think they want nothing to do with it. The educational program of the church can serve a valuable function by helping children, youth, and adults:

- Learn to comfortably talk about their own personal

encounters with Christ.

- Recognize the importance of reaching out to friends who are unchurched and develop styles of outreach which are comfortable.

- Become aware that being a good friend to others is part of the Christian life and that friendship is the foundation upon which meaningful outreach is best built.

- Understand that outreach can be as simple as just saying to a friend, neighbor, co-worker, or acquaintance: "I have a good time in my Sunday school class every week, and I think you'd like the people there. Would you like to come with me next week?"

- Become more comfortable with Bible study and with talking about religious issues and questions.

Many denominations offer study materials on faith sharing and evangelism. Find out what resources are available, and adapt them to your particular situation. You may also find some of the following strategies for classes and groups helpful, depending on the age level with which you are working.

Strategy One

Have group members complete statements like the following in their own words and then talk about the statements in pairs or triads:

God is ...

The Holy Spirit is ...

To me, Jesus Christ is ...

Salvation means ...

Heaven is ...

Hell is ...

Praying helps ...

Real love is ...

The church at its best is ...

I feel God's presence when ...

Worshiping in church helps me by ...

My faith in Christ has helped me ...

The most difficult time in my life was when ...

Strategy Two

Talk with the class or group about the following guidelines for witnessing and faith sharing:

(1) DO consciously identify friends who are not members of a church and give no indication of professing the Christian faith. Almost everyone knows some people in this category.

(2) DON'T attempt to "win" those who are already part of another church. Taking people from another church may benefit your own local church but doesn't build the kingdom of God.

(3) DO share what your relationship with Christ and your involvement in church mean to you at appropriate times in normal conversations. Let others know when Christ has helped you cope with a difficult situation.

(4) DON'T be caught with inconsistency between what you say and what you do. When there is a contradiction between what you claim to believe and how you live, people will judge you on the basis of your actions - and they will be judging the validity of your faith as well.

(5) DO build friendships with people you would like to win for the Christian faith. Your words about Christ will have the most meaning when addressed to people who know you care

about them.

(6) DON'T feel that you have to be an intimate friend of someone in order to invite that person to a Sunday school class, a church social, choir, or worship. A sincere, enthusiastic invitation will often be accepted, especially by persons who have recently moved to the community. (A longer term relationship is generally needed for personal sharing about the faith.)

(7) DO follow Christ's example in caring about other people. Reach out to the lonely, the handicapped, the troubled. Learn to be Christ's presence to others, and make it clear that your faith is what motivates you to care.

(8) DON'T feel that you must have all the answers to reach out to someone with a problem. In fact, you will often be able to give the greatest witness as you share your own times of weakness and struggle rather than trying to come across as though you have all the answers. Tell about a difficult experience of your own, and share how your faith helped you pull through that time. Don't be afraid to acknowledge your own mistakes and times of doubt. Affirm that Christ is with us no matter what happens.

(9) DO ask others to join you at church activities, and offer to provide transportation. People are far more likely to accept an invitation if you are asking them to come WITH you.

10) DON'T ask more than one or two people at a time to visit a church activity. You want to be able to focus your energy on the person you've invited, and you want it to be clear that the focus of your concern is on your regard for that person rather than on an effort to increase the strength of the church.

(11) DO practice talking about your faith with others. Completing statements like those listed in Strategy One can be one approach. You may also want to role play inviting others to church and sharing the faith with others.

(12) DON'T use religious cliches. Most people have grown weary of phrases like "Are you saved?" and "What would happen if you died tomorrow?" Use your own words, and speak in a way that is comfortable for you.

Strategy Three

Find out to what extent the atmosphere in your class or group is one which encourages people to invite guests, helps visitors feel comfortable, and encourages visitors to return. Have class or group members indicate the extent of their agreement or disagreement with each of the following statements by marking an X at the appropriate place on the line, and then talk about the items:

There's at least one meeting each year to which we actively encourage all group members to bring guests.

Strongly Agree   Strongly Disagree

We practice sharing our faith so that group members feel comfortable reaching out to others.

Strongly Agree   Strongly Disagree

Everyone in this group feels fully included in discussions and activities.

Strongly Agree   Strongly Disagree

When a new person attends our group for the first time, everyone is introduced and makes a conscious effort to remember the name of the new person.

Strongly Agree   Strongly Disagree

Most people who visit our group come back a second time.

Strongly Agree   Strongly Disagree

We usually spend a lot of time talking to visitors before and after the group time.

Strongly Agree   Strongly Disagree

Some persons, who have not moved out of town, have stopped attending our group within the past six months.

_____

Strongly Agree   Strongly Disagree

If a person quits coming to our group, we always follow up to find out what's wrong.

_____

Strongly Agree   Strongly Disagree

When someone visits our group, an active group member always reaches out to that person during the week by bringing cookies, inviting that person to share a drink or a meal, or in some other way expressing our interest in that person.

_____

Strongly Agree   Strongly Disagree

We conduct our group meetings in such a way that a visitor would readily see that our faith is important to us.

_____

Strongly Agree   Strongly Disagree

We acknowledge our doubts and problems with the faith in such a way that a visitor would not think we are acting like we "have all the answers."

_____

Strongly Agree   Strongly Disagree

Our group affirms people who share differences of opinion and ask questions.

_____

Strongly Agree   Strongly Disagree

Our group meetings always include a time of prayer to help us be aware of God's presence in our midst.

_____

Strongly Agree   Strongly Disagree

When a member of our group goes through a difficult time, we remember that person in prayer and reach out in whatever ways we can.

Strongly Agree   Strongly Disagree

Part Four:

Reaching Out
To Particular Groups

In Part Three, we looked at ways to increase attendance at Christian education programs and events.
Increased attendance almost always brings gains in
membership and financial support.

Part Four examines groups of people with needs to
which the church can and should respond. No
individual church, of course, can initiate new ministries to every group discussed; and the categories
presented here are by no means exhaustive of the
kinds of need which exist in every community. Hope-
fully the pages which follow will help you and your
church think through the kinds of people in your
own community to whom it's appropriate to reach
out. The reaching out is done in a spirit of concern
and service, but the results in many instances will be
increased attendance.

"But a Samaritan while traveling came near him; and when he saw him, he was moved with pity. He went to him and bandaged his wounds, having poured oil and wine on them. . . Which of these three, do you think, was a neighbor to the man who fell into the hands of the robbers?"

Luke 10:33, 34a, 36

The Lesson of the Samaritan

> **CONCEPT:** Effective Christian education focuses more on people than on programs.

In attempts to improve Christian education and evangelism, most of us have a tendency to search out new or different or more aggressive programs. Programs, however, only work if they meet the needs of people. The Word of God must be made flesh in the concern of Christians for others. Programs as such do not change lives or win new people to the Christian faith. Programs are the *means* by which people share with people.

The story of the Good Samaritan is familiar to almost all adult Christians, but we often fail to embody the central concepts of that parable in our own lives or in the church. The priest and the Levite had been trained by formal programs and realized the obligations of obedience to God's law. That knowledge was of no benefit to the injured man, whose life was saved by the Samaritan's compassion and action.

Many passages of Scripture can be used to emphasize the same concept: the Gospel is shared by the words and actions of people. The Bible is not a program handbook; it is God's word to people about how we should live in response to God's love.

To put new life into educational ministry, start by thinking about the lives of people rather than inventing new programs. Programs should respond to the needs of people, and the church should be concerned about ALL KINDS of people. The list which follows should help you think about persons within your church and your community. You may want to do some investigative work before assuming that people in the categories which follow are not represented in your community. Use these symbols:

IC Persons who are already active in your church
NC Persons who are present in the neighborhood or ministry area of your congregation but who are not in your church or at least not in numbers proportionate to their population in the community
NF Persons not found in your church or in your church's neighborhood or ministry area.

_____ Retired persons
_____ Divorced persons
_____ Young married couples
_____ Teenagers
_____ The deaf
_____ Persons with impaired mobility (confined to wheelchairs, severe arthritis, etc.)
_____ Persons with learning disabilities
_____ Single male adults
_____ Single female adults
_____ Persons who are wealthy
_____ Persons who are poor
_____ Persons with advanced degrees
_____ Persons with little formal education
_____ Parents of infants and small children
_____ Parents of teenagers
_____ College students
_____ Members of the military
_____ Voluntary service participants (VISTA, BVS, etc.)
_____ White people
_____ African Americans
_____ Asian Americans
_____ Hispanic people
_____ Native Americans
_____ Childless couples
_____ Alcoholics
_____ Persons who have to work on Sundays
_____ Persons who find it hard to mix with others and make new friends
_____ Persons who have obvious physical disfigurement
_____ Persons of different political views than most of the congregation
_____ Persons who disapprove of drinking and/or smoking
_____ Persons who drink and/or smoke
_____ Persons suffering from terminal illness

_____ Persons with a more liberal theology than most of your church's membership
_____ Persons with a more conservative theology than most of your church's membership
_____ Persons who are struggling to grow spiritually
_____ Persons who want to help the hungry and the homeless
_____ The hungry and the homeless
_____ Persons who dislike traditional worship services
_____ Persons who dislike contemporary worship services
_____ Persons who have an extremely high need for feedback on the volunteer work they do
_____ Persons who are afraid of crowds
_____ Persons who are opposed to any kind of church involvement in political affairs
_____ Persons who believe the church should be actively involved in political affairs
_____ Persons who want to participate in social activities which will help them make new friends
_____ Young parents who need child care in order to participate in worship services or Sunday school
_____ Single parents
_____ Families who want church activities which keep them together as a family (rather than dividing them by age and sex)
_____ Persons who are concerned about the welfare of animals
_____ Your addition: _____
_____ Your addition: _____

Work with the preceding checklist can help you identify gaps in your current efforts at reaching people. You should not hurry out to start a new program for each category which was marked **NC**. Remember that the focus should be on people. There is also a pragmatic limit on the number of new programs which a church can begin in any given period of time.

Some of the sections which follow will provide more information on reaching out to particular kinds of people. As you spend time thinking about the needs of people, you may come to some decisions like these:

1. The needs of people who share some common characteristics can best be met through special programs tailored to their needs and interests.
2. The needs of people often can best be met by involving them individually in groups which

117

   already exist in the church.
3. For a variety of reasons, your church may not be
   able to adequately meet the needs of every group
   or every person.
4. Even if you develop new programs, people become
   involved in those programs because others reach out
   to them. The programs alone will not do it!

Young Adults
and
The Push for Change

Concept: Churches which want to involve young adults in Christian education programs and in the congregation as a whole must be prepared to pay a price - and the price is change.

All across the United States and Canada, local churches are seeking to gain more young adult members. Some congregations are almost at the point of panic because they have so few young adult members in comparison to the numbers of young adults in their neighborhoods or ministry areas. As your church thinks about reaching out to particular categories of people, young adults will probably constitute one of the chief groups of concern.

Denominational and congregational definitions of "young adults" vary, but most commonly include those persons who are between the ages of eighteen and thirty-five. Some churches have raised the upper age limit to forty. Young adults can be found in a wide range of life situations:

Marital Status
- Single
- Married
- Divorced

Employment
- College or trade school students
- Armed Forces members
- Volunteer service participants

- Employed
- Unemployed

Parental Status
- Single with no children
- Married with no children
- Single with one or more children
- Married with one or more children

Residence
- Living in college housing
- Living with parents
- Living in an apartment
- Living in a single family residence

When leaders in most local churches think about starting a major emphasis on reaching more young adults, the mental image they hold is generally that of young adult families consisting of a husband, a wife, and two young children all living together in a single family residence, supported primarily by the employment of the husband. As you can readily see from the range of life situations just shared, young adults live in a far wider range than that stereotypical image.

There are many reasons why young adults are less likely to be active members of a local church now than in some past decades. Increased mobility means that they are not likely to remain in the congregation of their parents. They are also less likely to have loyalty to a particular denomination.

Baby boomers and the generations which have followed place great emphasis on personal fulfillment and are not as likely as older generations to join a local church from a feeling of obligation as from a conviction that their own needs will be well met through the life of the congregation. Many young adults are impatient with the slowness of the decision-making process in the typical church; as a result, they are not likely to become involved in leadership roles even if they do join the church. Consider the following comments from young adults:

"I go to church sometimes, but I can't find any fellowship there. I feel out of place. The church is always concerned about raising money for the building and for this program and that program... I can't take it. I keep feeling like all they want is my money and my work. I don't feel like I'm important to them as an individual... When I stay for coffee after worship services, people are friendly enough; but it's superficial. One older couple in the church have introduced themselves to me six times now. I remembered who they were after the first time. They would know who I was by now if they cared, but it's just a ritual with them." (23-year-old male)

"I can't see myself going to church. You can look at T.V. on Sunday morning and see what garbage people are fed. Give money to this, and God will bless you. Buy my book on prayer, and God will heal you... God isn't that narrow. I've always believed in God, but my God is more open. I've got my own faith, and my life is in order. I don't need the church." (29-year-old male)

"The last time I went to a meeting at church, we spent like forty or forty-five minutes deciding what kind of sandwiches to serve with the chili at a church supper. It takes forever for us to make any kind of decision. I don't have the patience. I care about the church, but it takes us too long to accomplish things." (33-year-old female)

"I'm a single parent. I didn't plan on being a single parent, but it just worked out that way. The church has always been important to me, but I find myself going less and less. People at our church are always talking about being one big family together. People probably don't mean it like it sounds, but I get the impression that there's something wrong with me because I don't have a husband. Mine was killed in an automobile accident, but I don't think I should have to explain that all the time. It shouldn't make any difference... I don't fit in with the singles' class because I'm the only one with a child. I sure don't fit with the couples' class, and a couple of the women in there look at me like they're afraid I'll try to steal their husbands. I don't think I've done anything that should make them feel uncomfortable, but I've gotten the message." (28-year-old female)

There are a wide range of strategies that can help a local church reach more young adults, and those are discussed more thoroughly in The Andrew Center Report *Fifty Ways to Reach Young Singles, Couples, and Families* by Steve Clapp. The following recommendations can help you in establishing more effective young adult programs through Christian education:

1. Most local churches need to focus on one or two categories of young adults and make a special effort to reach those persons. Programs designed primarily for young people who are college students will generally not be successful at integrating a number of non-college singles. Programs aimed at married couples are not likely to successfully integrate single parents. There's an upper limit on how many new classes or groups most local churches can initiate in one year. Your church may decide to focus on a group for single college students this year and then begin laying the foundation for a young couples group in the future.

2. If you want to reach significant numbers of young adults, then that age range needs to be well represented in the leadership of your church. You especially need to have young adult representation on your chief governing board, on the personnel or pastor-parish committee, and on the education committee (or whatever the appropriate terminology is within your denominational tradition). Be warned - the young adult members of those groups will want more rapid change than will probably have been the pattern in the past!

3. Young adult ministries are generally characterized by very high turnover. Graduation from college or trade school, the completion of a term in the armed forces or voluntary service, and opportunities for employment advancement can all make moves a necessity. Groups made up of young singles will inevitably go through change as some of those single persons decide to get married! Thus churches starting ambitious young adult outreach programs must be prepared to make transitions quickly. It's also important to involve young adult visitors and new members as early as possible in the life of the church because their tenure in the community may not be lengthy.

4. Older adults in the church need help understanding that there will be differences in values, opinions, and behaviors between themselves and younger adults who are potential members of the congregation. It's important to help them realize that building good relationships with young adults isn't the same thing as approving of all their behaviors. Relationship building can provide opportunities for values clarification and new discoveries of biblical truth.

5. Most young adults are searching for social outlets as well

as learning opportunities. A well-planned Christian education program for young singles or couples will provide opportunities to share meals, parties, recreational activities, service projects, and travel.

Many singles who move to new communities search almost desperately for social opportunities. If those can be found in the local church, they are willing to give considerable commitment to those activities.

6. Many young adults are surprisingly open to helping local churches plan classes and groups - if they sense that the interest of the church is genuine. In one study of more than a hundred singles who were not members of any local church, over three-fourths of the singles said they would be glad to talk with members of a church who were serious about establishing a singles ministry.   One of the most important steps in establishing new programs for young adults is to get them involved in the process.

7. The occasion of the birth of a child is an important one for all parents. That generally is a time when parents are especially open to the influence of the church. Many churches use those occasions as opportunities for special outreach to the parents. Volunteers bring a rose or another gift to the mother and offer whatever help may be needed. As increased mobility has many young adults several hundred miles away from their own parents, the concern of an older church member may be deeply appreciated. Some churches have begun the tradition of making small quilts for infants, and those are very well-received by the parents.

8. While it's true that young adults tend to be waiting a little longer to get married than has been the case in some earlier generations, the institution of marriage is still alive and well. Many local churches are finding significant outreach opportunities through:

- Marriage preparation retreats for couples who are engaged or who are considering becoming engaged.

- Marriage enrichment retreats for those who are already married.

- Seminars on financial management, which is one of

the leading causes of stress in the early years of a marriage.

9. Many churches are using their day care and nursery school programs as more effective "ports of entry" into the life of the church. Young adults who are bringing their children to the church for care generally feel good about the church. Those who did not have a church home often respond positively to invitations to become part of a class or group within the congregation. That can lead in time to church membership.

10. Many excellent Christian education programs for young adults are held at non-traditional times and settings. Here are some ideas that have worked for some congregations:

- Friday evening supper clubs meeting in restaurants, churches, and homes.

- 7 AM weekday Bible study groups which share rolls, juice, and coffee at the church or which meet at a restaurant near where many young adults work or attend classes.

- A group which meets on Saturdays to do service projects.

- A group which prepares a thirty minute program on community issues that is shown on a cable television station once a month.

- A support group that is itself the main counseling team for a youth program.

- A video club that meets at the church and in homes to view and discuss current videos.

- A group which provides friendship, help, and encouragement to single parents.

The Divorced and Others
Needing Support

Concept: People who have been through divorce and other difficult experiences need encouragement and support from the church.

Divorce has unquestionably become more commonplace in our society over the past twenty years. Some of the statistics cited about divorce, however, make the situation seem worse than it is. Several authorities have claimed that the divorce rate stands at 50%. They arrive at that figure by dividing the total number of marriages in a given year by the total number of divorces in that same year. For the past several years, it is true that there have been around half as many divorces as marriages, so that is taken as representing a 50% divorce rate. The logic doesn't stand up. Most of the divorces which occur in a given year don't involve the persons who got married in that same year! The number getting divorced must be seen in relationship to the total number of persons who are married. Divorce rates need to be calculated on the basis of the actual number of individual marriages which are terminated in that way.

The overall divorce rate in the United States currently stands at around 26%. That rate does seem to be moving in an upward direction, but it certainly is not at 50%. The fact that the statistical divorce rate has been exaggerated doesn't decrease the sorrow of God as covenants of marriage are broken. It also doesn't lower the pain which people experience as a result of relational failure. While divorce may at times appear a blessed end to a marriage which has become unbearable, divorce also brings a deep sense of loss and a questioning of personal worth.

Here are some insightful comments which divorced persons have shared:

"I can't believe Hank left me for someone so young. I thought everything was just fine. He was busy with his work, but that's nothing new. Then one day I find out that it's all over. I feel so stupid. I'm overweight. I'm picky and neurotic. I spend too much money. No wonder he left me. I feel out of place everywhere." (54-year-old female)

"The church doesn't condone divorce. I don't think I would want it to, but I feel excluded from so many things. The church says I'm forgiven, but I can't take communion. How can you be forgiven and still be barred from communion? I feel like I have to keep explaining and explaining." (26-year-old female)

"My marriage was horrible - at least the last two years were. I know a lot of it was my fault, though I had trouble accepting that for a long time. I'm scared to death to get into another marriage. I probably will, but how will I know that I won't cause the same thing again? Maybe I'll choose someone just like Sandy and make the same mistakes over and over." (34-year-old male)

"I know I have to start going out with people again, but it scares me. I don't know what to say. I haven't had to ask someone out for years.... I'm pretty old fashioned and don't know how well I'll be accepted by others. I don't even know how to go about meeting women. I haven't encountered any single women my age at the church. What should I do? Go to bars?" (32-year-old male)

"I need God so much. I need something to cling to. I've neglected my faith for years. Now I need it desperately, and I'm like a stranger to God. I think He's trying to get through to me, but I don't know how to hear what he says." (48-year-old male)

Guilt, anger, low self-worth, and the struggle for faith go along with divorce. Few crises in life present people with such a strong need for support through the church.

There are two ways in which a church can go about providing significant educational ministries to divorced persons. The first strategy is that of seeing that these persons are involved in ongoing classes and groups in the churches. Members of various church groups need to take the initiative in reaching out to divorced persons both within the church and the community. People going through the trauma of divorce often grow weary of explaining what has happened to everyone they encounter. They may also assume that people in the church have more negative feelings toward them than are actually present. Thus others in the church should take the initiative in reaching out to those dealing with divorce.

One of the problems is that the presence of a divorced person sometimes raises insecurities in those who are not divorced. "If that happened to him (or her), it could happen to me." In fact, persons may sometimes act as though divorce were a disease which could be caught. The presence of a divorced person can cause those who are married to reflect on all the flaws of their relationships and to wonder at what point divorce is actually an acceptable option.

But no one can escape the reality of divorce's presence in our society. Making divorced persons feel uncomfortable within the church does nothing to lower the divorce rate; it simply deprives those persons of the love and support which the church can provide and which has the power to transform lives.

The second strategy is that of forming a special group for those persons who have just gone through or who are still going through the trauma of divorce. If you want to begin such a group, it is **essential** that you involve a couple of persons who have gone through divorce in the planning process. Divorced persons are not going to attend a class or group which is under the leadership of someone who does not understand the hurt which they have experienced. Some churches provide leadership for such support groups by combining the efforts of the church's clergy with those of someone who has been through a divorce and who has made a reasonable adjustment to that reality.

Such groups do not have to be large. Four or five people may be sufficient for a valuable support group. If the group is to be of an ongoing nature, it's important that discussion not be limited to the topic of divorce. People must get about the business of living their own lives. The following format has been used successfully in several churches:

- Have a time of refreshments at the beginning of an evening meeting.

- Have introductions of any new persons present

127

followed by a brief business meeting in which social activities or service projects might be planned.

• Have a rotating schedule which provides for a speaker one week and a Bible study the next week. Speakers include doctors, attorneys, accountants, bankers, clergy, and others who can give helpful information and perspective to those dealing with divorce. The Bible study provides a needed spiritual dimension.

• Provide time for group members to share any joy or concerns which they've experienced during the week.

• Close with prayer.

The Death of a Loved One

The death of a loved one can be a horrible time and brings a huge number of problems to most people. If the death is that of a mate, then it is generally accompanied by a number of complicated legal, financial, and related issues. The death of a child often produces a crisis of faith, as those who've experienced the loss try to understand how God can permit such a tragedy. An increasing number of local churches are offering support groups to help those going through the pain of a death within the family.

Several such support groups have found meaning in studying resources like Leslie Weatherhead's **The Will of God**, Elisabeth Kubler-Ross's **Death - The Final Stage of Growth**, and Harold Kushner's **When Bad Things Happen to Good People**. Groups have also found it helpful to include visits with a psychologist who specializes in death and grief, a banker, an attorney, an insurance agent, and any other professionals who can share needed information.

Since the death of a loved one raises so many complex theological issues, it may be best for the minister to lead at least part of the discussions. Most people need considerable help in dealing with the reality of suffering, which many find inconsistent with God's love and the image of creation as good. A minister can give helpful guidance; share perspective related to

Christ's suffering, death, and resurrection; and assist people in accepting the reality that there may not be fully satisfactory answers to some of their questions. Grief is truly a process, and clergy as well as psychologists have experience in helping persons move through grief and recovery.

Ministers often perform funeral services for persons who are not members of the church, and congregational members will also know persons who have suffered a loss and have no church home. A support group can be an extremely valuable resource for those in the midst of the grief process, and it is appropriate to extend an invitation to persons who need that help. While involvement in such a group will sometimes result in a person becoming a member of the church, that should not be the primary motivation for reaching out with Christ's love and offering the support of caring people.

Other Support Groups

Many local churches have had considerable success offering a wide range of support groups in response to the needs of people in the church itself and in the neighborhood or ministry area served by the church. Successful groups have been formed to help persons:

- Who are single parents

- Who are striving to lose weight

- Who have addictions to alcohol or other drugs

- Who are going through serious discipline problems with a child or young person

- Who have a spouse who is incarcerated

- Who have been released from prison and are seeking to build a new life

- Who have been the victims of crime

- Who are unemployed

- Who have continuing problems with depression

129

- Who have adopted children

While you shouldn't attempt to start too many different groups at a time, there are marvelous opportunities to respond to human need with groups that may in time become ports of entry into the life of your congregation. Remember, however, that the primary motive must be that of genuine service and love in Christ's name rather than using such groups in a manipulative way.

Those Facing Difficult Challenges

Concept: The church needs to reach out to the physically and mentally challenged both for their sake and for the sake of the church.

A few years ago Steve Clapp visited with the Board of Education in a local church about possible ways of increasing membership in the Sunday school. When Steve asked who some of the physically handicapped persons were in the church and community, he received these responses:

"Well, we really don't have anyone who's handicapped in the church. We have a few who need a walker or a cane to get around. And we have some who don't hear so well or see so well, but they aren't really handicapped."

"We talked about putting in a wheelchair ramp a couple of years ago. We were supposed to put one in with the remodeling of the education building, but we managed to get around the building code. After all, we don't have anyone who uses a wheelchair... I guess that old Dr. Gruder needed a wheelchair, but we just carried him in the church. That was a lot cheaper than a ramp. Our congregation's like that. We'd carry anyone into our church who wanted to come."

"Sometimes I feel handicapped myself. Since my heart attack, I can't cope with stairs very well. I suppose we don't need it for wheelchairs, but I wouldn't mind a ramp for myself."

"Some of the people in the community are handicapped. I

don't think they go to church. They don't feel comfortable around normal people... I feel sorry for people like that, but I don't know how you could get them in the church."

The group was honest, and the responses are typical of those made in many churches. That church defined its ministry area (the area from which most of its members come and about which the congregation feels it should be most concerned) as a circle around the church with an eight mile radius. Further investigation revealed that within the ministry area:

- There are at least sixty people who communicate by sign language.

- There are at least 188 people who are confined to a wheelchair or who have mobility problems so great that a walker or cane is not sufficient to take them far.

- There are more people with serious heart conditions than anyone can accurately estimate.

- There are over a hundred children with different kinds of disabling conditions.

- There are at least twenty-one persons who are totally or partially blind.

- There are numerous other persons with handicaps that do not severely restrict their mobility but which can be recognized and make them self-conscious.

- There are at least sixteen people who are seeing a plastic surgeon for help with facial deformities.

And almost none of those persons, except the ones with heart conditions and a few with mobility problems, are actively involved in local churches. Consider some of their thoughts:

"People mean well. I know that they do. But people never see me. They see my handicap. I don't get angry about it anymore. It doesn't do any good. My neighbor tries to be friendly, but he avoids looking at my scar or prosthesis. We always talk across the fence, and we always talk about the weather. We invited them over to our house a couple of times, but there was always a reason why they couldn't come."

"Yes, I've had people from churches tell me that they'd be glad to help me get inside if I wanted to come. One person said that he'd be glad to carry me in. Another said that his church would put in a ramp if I were actually going to come... Look, folks, I don't want to be carried. I'm no baby. I have some pride. And I'm not about to be the reason that some church spends three or four thousand on a ramp. If you're not wanted somewhere, you don't go. And the churches don't want me."

"We want so much for our son to have a normal childhood. We'd do almost anything to make that possible. But the older he gets, the more he realizes how different he is. We don't take him to church. He wouldn't fit in. We need to protect him...
"I guess that's inconsistent with saying we want a normal childhood for him. That's the trouble with parenting a handicapped child - sorry, a physically challenged child is the right way to say it now. Anyway, you want things to be normal, but sometimes things just refuse to be normal. Maybe a family class would help - a class where we could go with him and where other people went with their children. Then we could help him bridge the gap...
"We should never have left Jackson. The kids there were used to him, and he had friends. I got a promotion with the move, and we have a better income now, but he's paid the price."

"Being deaf is very, very hard on a person. Gail has had a bad time. It's almost impossible to explain the frustration of not being able to make people understand that you can't understand... Sign language does help, but not enough people know it.
"We can't possibly bring her to church. She wouldn't understand anything that happened, and it would be very frustrating. No way. I don't blame the church. You can't sign a whole service for one child. I do know some communities that have a community-wide Christian program for the deaf. That would be nice. She at least needs to be in a CCD class soon."

The physically challenged are present in every community, but they are almost never present in the church to the same extent that they are in the community. There is a sense in which the physically challenged are not themselves a problem;

those of us who are able-bodied are the source of their problem. We look at them and see the handicap instead of seeing the person who happens to be disabled. That doesn't mean that we should take the seriousness of a person's handicap lightly, but it does mean that we should see the person before the handicap. Here are some starting points if you want to get serious about reaching out to the physically challenged:

1.   Create a task force or assign a specific group the task of finding ways to better work with the physically challenged. That task force should read Harold Wilke's ***Creating the Caring Congregation***. Wilke is himself handicapped, and he writes with compassion for both the handicapped and the able-bodied.

2.   Recognize that those who are able-bodied need the handicapped fully as much as the handicapped need interaction with the able-bodied. The handicapped have much to teach all of us. They have learned to cope with adverse conditions, and many have developed special gifts and abilities.

Those who are able-bodied need to reach sufficient understanding and comfort that being around the physically challenged is not disconcerting. In response to Christ's love, we are obligated to see the person made in God's image before us. Focusing overly on the handicap keeps us from recognizing others as our brothers and sisters in Christ. The absence of the physically challenged from our congregations, our sanctuaries, and our Christian education programs stands as an indictment that we have rejected the presence of our Lord. We need to be set free from the anxieties and fears which separate the abled and the disabled. That cannot be done unless we have contact with the physically challenged.

3.   In most instances, the physically challenged do not need special classes or groups. Those with problems of mobility do need to be able to enter and move around the church as conveniently as possible, and the disabled need to feel accepted in the total life and program of the church.

4.   If no other church in your community offers programs for the deaf, then a special program for that group may well be in order both in Christian education and in worship.

5.   It is especially valuable to reach out to physically challenged children. The abled and the disabled mix far more

naturally as young children than later in life. Levels of comfort and strong relationships established during the early years of life can be very valuable later.

6. Seek the help of persons who are physically challenged in reaching out to others. If these persons are part of the planning process, you are far more likely to reach out with success.

7. Seek help in identifying the physically challenged in your community. Many church members will know persons who are physically challenged. You can also be in contact with schools, vocational rehabilitation centers, hospital physical therapy departments, and physicians. Be sure to emphasize that you are not wanting to pressure or sell anything to the physically challenged. Agencies which give special services to the handicapped will not want to violate the confidentiality of those persons, but they can make information available if they are convinced of the sincerity of your concern. They can often help provide training programs for Sunday school or CCD leaders and others who may be working with physically challenged persons.

For Those Who Have Problems Learning

Some people learn more quickly than others. That's a fact of life. Our society has come a long way in understanding why people have trouble learning and in finding ways to help, but we still have far to go.

The jargon covering this area is immense, and the correct terminology keeps changing: mentally-challenged, learning-challenged, trainable-mentally-handicapped, educable-mentally-handicapped, dyslexic, learning-disabled, mildly-retarded, profoundly-retarded, special students, and so the categories continue. Most of us never catch up because the terminology changes so often, and philosophies about the best ways of providing educational help to these persons also change. Special classes are used for some; special tutoring may be provided for others.

You can be certain that there are persons with serious learning problems in your community. The public school system can generally give you a good idea of the number of children and young people with various kinds of learning problems.

Whether your church should cooperate in an ecumenical program, offer a special class of its own, or attempt to integrate persons with learning problems into regular Sunday school or CCD classes is difficult to determine. The answer depends on the number of those persons not being served currently and on the nature of the challenges which they face. In general, the more normal the environment which can be provided for them, the better. Use the expertise of persons in your community who work with the physically challenged and those with learning problems in the public schools and seek guidance from the offices of your denomination.

Reaching Teenagers

> **Concept:** Growth in a church's youth program can come through improvements to existing groups and also through the addition of new groups.

Reaching young people has always been a vital component of local church programming, but its importance has become even greater in recent years:

- More congregations are experiencing significant difficulty retaining teenagers after they have been formally confirmed into the church.

- While use of some illicit drugs seems to have declined, problems with alcohol have increased.

- Teenage sexual activity continues at a high rate with more and more teenage parents choosing to keep their children.

- Far more teenagers are involved in criminal activity, including violent crimes such as homicide.

- Depression, eating disorders, and suicide destroy the lives of many young people.

Our local churches continue to fall into the trap of doing youth programming primarily on the basis of models which were developed many years ago. When our society was more rural in nature and lacking in community activities for young people, the motivation to attend a church youth group was much higher. Today, most communities have ever-increasing numbers of school, scout, YMCA, YWCA, athletic, and music programs. The opportunities for motion pictures, bowling, skating, shopping, and eating out are readily available to teens; and many have part-time jobs to earn the money for those activities and to save for college.

Many churches have Sunday evening youth fellowships because "there has always been one" and "teenagers need to be in the church." Such reasons are not precise and are not always adequate justification for the existence of a program.

If you want to reach out more successfully to young people, then you need to take a careful look at the youth in your church and in your community. You may decide to continue your existing opportunities, but you may also identify some new strategies. If your church does not already have a Youth Council or similar group for overall review of your youth program, consider appointing a special task force to evaluate your current programs and make recommendations for the future.

Such a task force should include the minister, a few adults who work directly with youth (teachers, music directors, or group advisors), a few parents, and several young people. The exact numbers will depend on your situation. Some churches do not have "several" young people. You may wish to ask one or two inactive teenagers or even some youth in the community who have no church home to be part of the task force. The Youth Council or task force should:

- Identify the existing programs for youth and how many persons are served by those programs. What is the average attendance of each group? What are the strong points? The weak points?

- Interview young people who are on the task force and also young people who are served by your church but are not on the task force. Find out how they view the existing youth program and what needs they have which are not currently being met.

- Interview several teens in the community who do not belong to your church to gain their insight. Find out whether or not they are involved in another church. If they were once active and have become inactive, find out why. Ask them to

share the kinds of programs or activities which
would interest them in your church; you may
need to give them several choices. Keep track
of responses to help you in decision making.
Those teens who do not have church homes may
be prospective members for your church.

•   Visit with adults who work with teenagers who
    are experiencing trouble with drugs, alcohol,
    eating disorders, depression, and criminal
    activity. Ask the adults for help in determining
    the kinds of programs which your church might
    successfully offer.

Take the information generated by the preceding activities
and then make decisions about the areas of need which you
wish to target with your youth program. As you think about
possibilities, remember that very few youth groups grow larger
than twenty young people in average attendance unless several
adults are working with them. Quality programming is important, but close relationships are what make youth groups grow.
The nurturing of those relationships and proper follow-up on
those who stop coming demand considerable adult time. Large
youth groups must be broken into small groups for the purposes
of study and sharing, and one or two adults are needed for each
of those small groups. If you have potential for reaching a larger
number of young people, then you need to consider adding
teachers (for Sunday morning) or advisors (for Sunday evening) -
or adding new groups. Responding to questions such as the
following may help you determine whether or not you need new
groups:

1. Do young people tend to become inactive in your church
when they reach a certain age? If so, you may need a group that
will appeal more to older teens. High school seniors have
different interests and concerns than freshmen.

2. Does the same group span both junior high and senior
high young people? If so and if there are enough young people in
your church, you may want to create separate groups for junior
high youth and for senior high youth. Combining these age
levels is possible, but should be done only when there is no
realistic alternative.

3. Do you have young people who want a more serious opportunity for Bible study, prayer, and spiritual growth? By all means start a group for them rather than have them become church dropouts.

4. Do your young people and others in your ministry area have interests and needs which are not met adequately in the community? Funding problems have caused many school districts to eliminate drama, art, and music programs. They can be an appropriate means of expressing the Christian faith, and you may be able to capitalize on the failure of the public schools to supply these opportunities.

5. Do young people in your church have special interests? Some Youth Councils have started movie groups which meet weekly to view and discuss a movie in a theater or on a VCR. Some churches have formed groups of teens to prepare a weekly or monthly program to be broadcast on a local cable channel.

6. Are there needs of youth in the community which could be met through programs offered by your church? Possibilities include sexuality education classes, self-esteem building groups, and conflict resolution groups. You may be able to get the media and community leaders to help you publicize these opportunities.

Short-term interest groups can be a good strategy in many churches. Every church and community will have young people who are simply not able or willing to commit themselves to a Sunday school class or fellowship group for months at a time. In adult work, churches have long recognized the value of short-term Bible study, prayer, and interest groups. Many churches offer adults opportunities like marriage enrichment, Bible study, mission groups, and heritage classes for specified amounts of time - generally four to ten weeks. Some persons will join a group in which they have a special interest much more readily than a traditional class.

In most churches it's much easier to integrate new teens into new groups than into existing groups. Interest groups can involve a mixture of previously active and inactive young people. This contact can prove very healthy.

If you decide to begin one or more new groups, then go back to the young people in your own church and in the community with whom you visited when conducting the youth program evaluation. Explain that you now have a new opportunity in response to the needs and ideas which were shared with you, and seek to involve each of those young people in what you do.

Don't be discouraged if your church is so small that you only have five or six young people. Focus on those young people. Find out what they need and want from the church and from life itself. You may only have one group or class, but that group will be successful if it really starts with the needs of your young people. You may be able to expand opportunities by cooperating with another church or churches.

A Reminder!

From the beginning, this book has emphasized the reality that effective outreach includes both of these dimensions:

- Sharing the faith with those outside the church and inviting them to become part of the body of Christ.

- Sharing the faith by responding to the needs of persons outside the church as well as those who are already part of the Christian community.

Successful youth outreach, like outreach to children and adults, will include both dimensions. Our society has growing concern about the needs of youth, and a vital youth program in your church can be a means of reaching both teenagers and their parents with the good news of Jesus Christ.

Resources

The books listed below are available from The Andrew Center. Send your order to The Andrew Center, 1451 Dundee Avenue, Elgin, Illinois 60120, or call 1-800-774-3360.

Riding the River - *Congregational Outreach and the Currents of the 21st Century* by Paul Mundey. Paul Mundey examines some of the most significant changes projected for our society and explores the implications of those transitions for the local church. Includes study questions for use by church planning groups, boards, and classes. R2004 $5.95

Fifty Ways to Reach Young Singles, Couples, and Families by Steve Clapp. Almost every local church desperately wants to reach more young adults. This practical report, based on Steve Clapp's extensive experience consulting and working with congregations of all sizes, offers tested, practical ways for reaching out. R2006 $6.95

Overcoming Barriers to Church Growth by Steve Clapp. Let's face it - 20 years of church growth programs, promotions, rallies, books, videos, conferences, and resolutions haven't reversed the trend of decline in most mainline churches. Pastors and laity are frustrated because so much hard work has resulted in so little real change. In *Overcoming Barriers to Church Growth*, Steve Clapp confronts the attitudes and barriers to growth which church leaders face. R2010 $12.95

Youth Workers Handbook by Steve Clapp and Jerry O. Cook is a popular resource which has been completely revised and is PACKED with strategies for improving your church's youth program and reaching new teenagers. Practical, easy-to-follow ideas for evangelism, fellowship groups, retreats, camps, classes, videos, service projects, and recreation. R2061 *$16.95*

Peer Evangelism: Youth and the Big, Scary 'E' Word by Steve Clapp and Sam Detwiler offers practical, nonmanipulative strategies to help teens reach the unchurched. This book faces the reality that youth are uncomfortable with evangelism and shows them how they can share their faith and reach out in comfortable ways. Thirteen sessions plus permission to photocopy. R2062 *$16.95*

Christian Education in the Small Church by Donald L. Griggs and Judy McKay Walther shares how to have effective Christian education in small churches - including strategies for growth. R2063 *$9.95*

44 Ways to Expand the Teaching Ministry of Your Church by Lyle Schaller, the man the *Los Angeles Times* called "America's most influential religious leader," shows why teaching is one of the most effective ways to attract new members, especially young adults. R2064 *$10.95*

Ministry with Young Adults - The Search for Intimacy edited by Julie Garber is a practical handbook for churches wanting to attract young adults (ages 18-35) and involve them in the faith community. Explores the needs of young adults and how to meet those needs through classes, groups, retreats, and leadership roles. R2065 *$7.95*

Developing Faith in Young Adults by Robert T. Gribbon shares information from more than a decade of research into the search of young adults for integrity and faith. R2068 *$11.95*

The titles which follow are not available from The Andrew Center, but we also strongly recommend these materials:

Building a Great Children's Ministry by Evelyn M.R. Johnson and Bobbie Bower is an excellent book on reaching today's children. *Abingdon.*

The Vital Singles Ministry by Harry Odum describes the Phoenix Sunday School Class which grew to 1,200 single persons in weekly attendance. *Abingdon.*

Rethinking Christian Education, edited by David S. Schuller, gives the results of the major Search Institute study of Christian education and is filled with valuable insights. *Chalice Press.*

Sunday Schools that Dared to Change by Elmer L. Towns shares the strategies of ten Sunday schools that experienced significant growth. *Regal Books.*

Shared Faith by Thomas H. Groome is a landmark book on Christian education as it relates to all aspects of the local church. This book has had great influence on curriculum development and seminary work across the country. *HarperCollins.*

Needing, Kneeling, Knowing by Judy Gattis Smith is a beautiful collection of devotions and exercises for the spiritual development of Sunday school teachers. *Discipleship Resources.*

Christian Education Made Easy by Howard Hanchey gives pragmatic guidance to building a strong Sunday school program. *Morehouse Publishing.*

About the authors:

Steve Clapp is a writer and church consultant in the areas of church growth, youth work, and Christian education. He has authored or coauthored over twenty books including *Peer Evangelism, Christian Education as Evangelism, Youth Workers Handbook, Promising Results,* and *Overcoming Barriers to Church Growth.* He is Senior Consultant to The Andrew Center and is involved in several continuing research projects related to congregational outreach.

Jerry O. Cook is pastor of the United Methodist Church in Framingham, Massachusetts. He was for many years an editor at the United Methodist Publishing House, and he has had extensive involvement in the development of a wide range of curriculum resources. He is the author of the books *Worship Resources for Youth, Through the Bible - Volume III,* and *Youth Workers Handbook.*